AN EARNEST BLACKNESS

AN EARNEST BLACKNESS

EUGEN BACON

An Earnest Blackness
Copyright © 2023 by Eugen Bacon
ISBN: 979-8-98-654795-4
Library of Congress Control Number: 2023947890

First Anti-Oedipal Paperback Edition, November 2023

www.rawdogscreaming.com

Cover Design & Layout © 2023 by D. Harlan Wilson
www.dharlanwilson.com

X @AntiOedipusP
IG @antioedipuspress

Anti-Oedipus Press
Grand Rapids, MI

www.anti-oedipuspress.com

BOOKS BY EUGEN BACON

Fiction

Black Moon: Graphical Speculative Flash Fiction
Broken Paradise
Chasing Whispers
Claiming T-Mo
Danged Black Thing
Hadithi & The State of Black Speculative Fiction (with Milton Davis)
Her Bitch Dress
It's Folking Political
Ivory's Story
Mage of Fools
Saving Shadows
Secondhand Daylight (with Andrew Hook)
Serengotti
Speculate (with Dominique Hecq)
The Road Woop Woop and Other Stories

Nonfiction

Writing Speculative Fiction

ACKNOWLEDGEMENTS

Acknowledgement is made to the following publications in which some of the essays in this collection first appeared:

"Afrofuturism: A WorldCon Recap, and Some Thoughts." *Vector Magazine*. August 2020.

"An Earnest Blackness." *Vector Magazine*. June 2021.

"Becoming Visible: The Rise of Black Speculative Fiction." *Vector Magazine*. May 2020.

"I Went Looking for AfroSF." *Vector Magazine*. May 2020.

"Inhabitation—Genni and I." *Sydney Review of Books*. November 2020.

"On Slipstream: A Personal View." *Aurealis* #141. May 2021.

"The Benefit of Our Humanity." *The Blue Nib*. June 2020.

"Worldbuilding in Ngũgĩ wa Thiong'o's *The Perfect Nine: The Epic of Gĩkũyũ and Mũmbi*." *Worlds Apart: Worldbuilding in Fantasy and Science Fiction*. Luna Press Publishing, 2021.

CONTENTS

THIS IS NOT A PREFACE

In *A Thousand Plateaus* (1980), Gilles Deleuze and Félix Guattari introduced the rhizome to the world. A rhizome "has no beginning or end; it is always in the middle, between things, interbeing, *intermezzo*" (25). The main elements of the rhizome are heterogeneity and (inter)connections that form a dialectic multiplicity. The rhizome has no center. It spreads continually from beginning to end. It adapts. It deviates. Most importantly, it decodes normative, culturally inscribed structures.

Text can be an open and connectable map; well achieved, it's a flexible composite—detached, reversible, variant. There is no subscribed order by which to read the miscellany of distinct yet interconnected essays collected in *An Earnest Blackness*, which rejects the idea of a stable, fixed self. I am a black writer, and black writing is evolving. Readerly perceptions are evolving. Knowledge is evolving—and knowledge is rhizomatic by default, offering infinite possibilities.

Our experiences inform how we write and how we perceive ourselves and others. Narrative is a crucial device to explore and facilitate the nature of being and inhabitation, the self and the "other." These essays—some of which are borrowed from lived experience—interrogate black writing and black speculative fiction, including the works of Ngũgĩ wa Thiong'o, Toni Morrison, Octavia Butler, Samuel R. Delany, Nisi Shawl, and Sheree Renée Thomas. *An Earnest Blackness* also considers some aspects of critical and cultural theories.

Additionally, this book investigates subgenres of black speculative fiction, among them cyberfunk, blacktastic, steamfunk, dieselfunk, black-tech, rococoa, and blaxploitation. In its earnest conversation on current issues and opportunities facing black writers today, coupled with its themes on writing the "other" betwixt hauntings, colonization, and unlimited futures, I hope these essays will be valuable resources for creators, commentators, and scholars of Afrofuturism, other African diasporic formations, and all textual variants that break boundaries.

References

Deleuze, Gilles and Fèlix Guattari. *A Thousand Plateaus.* 1980. Trans. Brian Massumi. University of Minnesota Press, 1987.

AN EARNEST BLACKNESS

Decades after the groundbreaking work of authors such as Toni Morrison, Samuel R. Delany, and Octavia Butler, black speculative fiction is more visible and thriving than ever. Through invented worlds, technologies, and incursions of the supernatural or the uncanny, more and more black speculative-fiction authors are offering stories of curiosity, diversity, hope, possibilities, probabilities, even dire warnings about our place in the universe.

There's power in this mode of writing. In a continued response to global events, these authors are increasingly curious and experimental, writing across genres in a rise of future forms to tell radical tales that speak to our curiosities, to lost or forgotten cultures, to decolonizing language, and to deconstructing and reconstructing self and identity.

The first African American woman to win the Nobel Prize in literature, Toni Morrison, saw narrative as radical. She wrote revolutionary stories, including the Pulitzer Prize-winning *Beloved* (1987), with its unsettling scrutiny at the awful legacy of slavery and a black woman forced to make a terrible choice, and *Song of Solomon* (1998), a genre-bending novel that bridges literary and speculative genres as well as themes of resilience and belief. "What difference do it make if the thing you scared of is real or not?" asks Morrison in the latter novel (41). "If you surrendered to the air, you could ride it" (337). *Song of Solomon* culminates with protagonist Milkman's leap, a surrender to the air so he can ride it. And now, more than ever, people of color are increasingly adopting black speculative fiction in stories of possibility so that they, too, can surrender to the air and ride it.

Black speculative fiction gives voice to the complex and varied experiences of African and Afro-descendant peoples. What Africa means, above all, is diversity, encompassing 54 countries, abundant languages (including Swahili, Amharic, Yoruba, Oromo, Hausa, Igbo, Zulu, Shona, and over 2,000 more), and 1.378 billion peoples. And that's just on the continent, before you factor in the diaspora, which refers to people whose ancestors migrated or were snatched from Africa (anyone of African descent in Europe, North America, South America, Asia, the Antarctica, Australia, Oceania, and elsewhere). Black speculative fiction confronts the colonial gaze, which tries to see only uniformity and sameness.

Even so, across so much of this vast diversity—these many unique languages, cultures, and stories; these many complex histories and power relationships—there are unifying threads. Perhaps the most important of these threads are anti-colonial and anti-racist movements, such as Black Lives Matter. Movements to build better worlds draw us together in a collective endeavor of re-imagining past and present experiences while exploring what black futures could look like.

One reason why Ryan Coogler's 2018 *Black Panther* struck such a chord was the way it evoked real colonial histories within a fantastical setting. The movie's villain,

Killmonger, speaks truths about the ongoing legacy of co-colonialism seldom heard in the context of a big Hollywood blockbuster. This Afrofuturist movie celebrates people of color via themes of racism, feminism, inclusion, and social injustice. The Force also awakens in Prince T'Challa of Wakanda (and his personal guard of Xhosa-speaking warrior women) in Titan's 2021 *Black Panther: Tales of Wakanda,* edited by Jesse J. Holland. Stories in this anthology host the many faces of T'Challa, who personifies the regal dignity of black people in eighteen brand-new tales of Wakanda, its people, and its legacy. "These are the tales of a king and his country," says the back-cover copy. "These are the legends whispered in the jungle, myths of the unconquered men and women and the land they love. These are the Tales of Wakanda." The anthology features short fiction by Linda D. Addison, Maurice Broaddus, Christopher Chambers, Milton J. Davis, Tananarive Due, Nikki Giovanni, Harlan James, Danian Jerry, Kyoko M., L.L. McKinney, Temi Oh, Suyi Davies Okungbowa, Glenn Parris, Alex Simmons, Sheree Renée Thomas, Cadwell Turnbull, and Troy L. Wiggins. Their stories speak to longing, heritage, and discovery—a reliving of Wakanda in tales that bridge Mother Africa and her diaspora.

With its brand-new tales of a kingdom, her people, and her legacy, *Tales of Wakanda* blends technology, jungle, nobility, gods, duty, heroes, antiheroes, kindred, and honor to celebrate black comic books, writers, and artists through vehicles of colonialism and postcolonialism. Poignant stories include "Heart of a Panther" by Sheree Renée Thomas, whose textual beauty and sensitivity takes us to ancient groves long after the weeping time; this rich, layered story about a vital journey to Mississippi investigates the shrivel of sacred herbs that are crucial to the

Rite of the Panther. In "Of Rights and Passage" by Danian Darrell Jerry, T'Swuntu voyages to Boston to find his lost son, but he finds much more in a world of slaves. Suyi Davies Okungbowa's "Stronger in Spirit" sees T'Challa struggle with an extraterrestrial autoimmune disease and go undercover in Lagos to commune with Bàbálúayé, a foreign healing god. Here T'Challa has the opportunity to compare Lagos with his own Golden City: "As often when I ride through these streets, I think of the stark difference with Birnin Zana's Vibranium-driven transport infrastructure and wonder how it may be of use here. All this energy on display could be put to better use if everyone wasn't so involved in a race for survival, where those who blink for too long get relegated to the background" (458).

In 2019, Okungbowa, whose writing on blackness across the diaspora takes all forms, released his award-winning *David Mogo Godhunter*, a novel in which Lagos succumbs to ruin when the gods fall. In this riveting debut, Okungbowa depicts a new Lagos. He released another novel in 2021, *Son of the Storm*, the first in a fantasy trilogy called The Nameless Republic in which a young scholar's ambition threatens Bassa, a colony, and her leadership's supremacy. With its politics, superstition, magical realism, greed, and revenge, *Son of the Storm* brings Africa alive in culture, in place (the Savanna Belt, the Idjama desert, the Breathing Forest, Whudasha), in language (phrasings in an African dialect), and in food (yams, palm wine, jackalberry, baobab porridge). Okungbowa's inversions of patriarchy and colonialism, where women hold positions of authority and black is power, are radical.

Son of the Storm adds to the climbing wave of black writing in all its future forms, genres, and modes—writing that's a warning and a promise, writing that's about black people taking ownership to reimagine their worlds. The novel's rawness and urgency extends to the works of writers like Toni Morrison, Octavia E. Butler, Nalo Hopkinson, Chinua Achebe, Wole Soyinka, Camara Laye, and Ngũgĩ wa Thiong'o.

Colonialism destroys and undervalues people's culture— their literature, their art, their dance, their philosophy, their religion, their science and technology. It nurtures betrayal, amplifies discord. It exposes the colonial child to a world where everything they know is now bad or inferior— Okwonkwo, our tragic hero in Chinua Achebe's *Things Fall Apart* (1958), discovered this truth in the harshest possible way. In *Decolonising the Mind: The Politics of Language in African Literature* (1986), Ngũgĩ writes:

> We spoke Gĩkũyũ in the fields. We spoke Gĩkũyũ in and outside the home. I can vividly recall those evenings of storytelling around the fireside. It was mostly the grown-ups telling the stories but everybody was interested and involved. We children would re-tell the stories the following day to other children … And then I went to school, a colonial school, and this harmony was broken. The language of my education was no longer the language of my culture … one of the most humiliating experiences was to be caught speaking Gĩkũyũ in the vicinity of the school. The culprit was given corporal punishment—three to five strokes of the cane on bare buttocks—or was made to carry a metal plate around the neck with inscriptions such as I AM STUPID or I AM A DONKEY. (548-49)

One of Ngũgĩ's early defiances was to denounce his British-ruled Kenyan name James Thiong'o Ngugi. His oeuvre asks crucial questions and contributes to the fight against colonialism, which robs the colonized of name, language, community, and value.

Decolonising the Mind is a firm but earnest conversation that once-colonized people will understand. Colonialism turns diversity into division and strife (divide and rule is a colonialist dictum), and it fosters violent instability. Colonialism operates both in the external world and the mind, stripping away language, community, and culture—where culture is food, family, clothing, housing, belief, ways of doing, and ways of seeing.

Speculative fiction, as a paradigm shift, comes with power inherent in its surreal or abstract nature. This type of fiction is a safe space to explore confronting themes and understand others' perspectives. Imagined worlds are an escape; they put you—a mind traveler to mythical worlds—at ease. There, you can explore outer space, inner space, climate change, racism, sexuality, social injustice, and an excess of dysfunction in the world as we know it.

Speculative fiction is a response to the universe and our place in it. We can ask fundamental philosophical questions. We can interrogate the past and learn from it.

We can contemplate different, better futures.

References

Achebe, Chinua. *Things Fall Apart*. Heinemann, 1958.

Holland, Jesse J. et al. *Black Panther: Tales of Wakanda*. Titan Books, 2021.

Morrison, Toni. *Song of Solomon*. Vintage Books, 1998.

———. *Beloved*. Alfred A. Knopf, 1987.

Ngũgĩ wa Thiong'o. *The River Between*. Heinemann, 1965.

———. *Petals of Blood*. Heinemann, 1977.

————. *Decolonising the Mind: The Politics of Language in African Literature.* 1986. Heinemann, 2011.

Okungbowa, Suyi Davies. *David Mogo Godhunter.* Abaddon Books, 2019.

————. *Son of the Storm.* Orbit, 2021.

WORLDBUILDING IN NGŨGĨ WA THIONG'O'S
THE PERFECT NINE: THE EPIC OF GĨKŨYŨ AND MŨMBI

"Life has and has not a beginning. Life has and has not an end. The beginning is the end and the end is the beginning." —*The Perfect Nine*

Creating imaginary worlds is essential in all forms of speculative fiction, whether the work is a novel or a short story. It is an investment that compounds the credibility of the work for readers. Richly invented worlds, made-up languages, visionary topography, and ingenious perspectives teleport us to infinite possibilities inside the fictional realms of an author's inventiveness.

Ngũgĩ wa Thiong'o's *The Perfect Nine: The Epic of Gĩkũyũ and Mũmbi* is a grand narrative about the founding of the nine clans of the Gĩkũyũ people of Kenya. This essay explores worldbuilding through creation mythology, culture, nature, and the otherworldly while blending folklore, adventure, and allegory. Ngũgĩ frames an accessible, large-scale, metaphoric world in this lush chronicle about the genesis of Gĩkũyũ clans. The success of the book validates him as a leading literary African author and scholar, a recipient of twelve honorary doctorates, and a nominee for the Man Booker International Prize.

Introducing the Novel

Ngũgĩ's black speculative fiction is a translation of its original Gĩkũyũ version titled *Kenda Mũiyũru* (2018). *The Perfect Nine* is a quest narrative that reimagines the mythology of Gĩkũyũ and Mũmbi, the respective "Adam and Eve" of the Gĩkũyũ people, one of the forty-two tribes in Kenya, East Africa (Gĩkũyũ).

The novel follows the mythic structure that Christopher Vogler explores in *The Writer's Journey* (1998), interrogating the relationship between mythology and storytelling. Vogler borrows this template from Joseph Campbell, who, in *The Hero with a Thousand Faces* (1949), adopted Carl Jung's theories of archetypes and the collective unconscious. Campbell recounts everything from the hero's call to adventure to his or her triumphant return. In *The Perfect Nine*, however, there's not one but many hero/ines, as ninety-nine suitors embark on a quest rife with trials and tribulations to win the hands of nine (plus one) daughters of the male Gĩkũyũ and female Mũmbi.

The story starts with the ordinary world in which these originary parents survive their own creation and hurdles to reach their home in a place called Mũkũrũweinĩ. They actually have ten (not the titular nine) daughters, all of them mature for marriage. Wanjirũ, Wambũi, Wanjikũ, Wangũi, Waithĩra, Njeri, Mwĩthaga, Wairimũ, Wangarĩ, and Warigia have grown without brothers and don't need men to complete them. Despite their self-sufficiency, they understand the trinity of life: birth, existence, and death. Each daughter has a role to build a clan, and suitors aren't lacking. Handsome young men arrive from far afield, lured by the silhouettes of the beautiful girls in their dreams; they lead them down valleys to rivers with song. In a feast of music and dance, the suitors perform their own unique rituals, some of which they picked up along the way. Gĩkũyũ and Mũmbi place upon the suitors many challenges. Initially, these challenges are meek: building a hut in one day, finding the daughters hidden in a black forest, making clothes from slaughtered animal skin, shooting an arrow in the eye of a tree at climbing distance. The remainder must go on a final, two-fold challenge: to travel to the mountain of the moon, to catch a piece of the moon in a gourd and mix it with water from the lake, and to find the cure-all hair of the unseen king of the human-eating ogres—healing hair that grows in the middle of the ogre's tongue. This cure-all will restore Warigia, the unspoken tenth, born with a disability.

Typical of the quest narrative, some suitors refuse the call to adventure. Those who accept it find that they must rely on the daughters to serve as mentors as they cross thresholds—and overcome obstacle after obstacle—to complete their quest. But once they achieve the treasures, there's an ordeal to make it back. The journey home is equally perilous, and many die. Finally, only ten suitors remain, one man for each daughter.

For those who have read Ngũgĩ's fiction—*Wizard of the Crow* (2006), *Petals of Blood* (1977), *The River Between* (1965)—seen his plays like *The Black Hermit* (1963), or read his essays and memoirs, the Unexpected is a common trope. Having overcome the novel's arrival in verse form, there's a whole new world for readers to immerse themselves in, process, and interpret. Herein lies the author's critical role of worldbuilding.

The Importance of Worldbuilding

Creating imaginary worlds is essential in all forms of speculative fiction.

In *How to Write Science Fiction and Fantasy* (1990), Orson Scott Card speaks to the importance of worldbuilding in hooking the reader: "Many readers, having once discovered a strange world that they enjoy, want to return to that same world again and again, until they're more familiar with that imaginary place than they are with the real-world town they live in" (24).

Assigning a whole chapter on world creation, Card emphasizes the importance of making rules for the invented world, rules that do not obstruct the reading experience but open possibilities and make the new world credible, however removed from the reality it might be. Worldbuilding of this nature involves evolution, history, culture, language, biography, and relatability.

In an analysis of Peter Stockwell's *The Poetics of Science Fiction* (2000) called "Who Framed Science Fiction," Istvan Csicsery-Ronay Jr. says SF specializes in producing large-scale metaphoric structures that engage readers through the author's architecture of a rich, textual universe; and this universe has the capacity to map readers' reality (125). In short fiction, worldbuilding need not be elaborate, if one goes with Raymond Carver's approach to writing the short form as "Get in, get out. Don't linger. Go on." Capable writers, however, take the time to develop setting in their speculative worlds, big or small.

In his novel, Ngũgĩ applies numerous literary devices to achieve effective worldbuilding.

Worldbuilding through Creation Mythology

Ngũgĩ writes: "Making things is a matter of hands and eyes. All my daughters are makers of things" (70). The novel borrows from folklore on the founding of Gĩkũyũ clans that begot a nation. The god of the mount, who is also the supreme giver and god of many names (e.g., Mulungu, Umvelinqangi, Nyasai, Jok, Ngai, Yahweh, and Allah), is a he/she unifying divinity. The giver puts Gĩkũyũ and Mũmbi at the top of the snow-capped Mount Kenya (like the Garden of Eden) and they survey the surrounding landscape.

They stand in awe at the summit, "white and massive as the moon" (5), and gaze at undulating plains, hills, valleys, rivers that flow through lilies. As they take in grass plains populated by giraffes, gazelles, zebras, antelopes, buffalos, lions, ostriches, and partridges, and as they listen to chirping birds all around the mountain, Gĩkũyũ and Mũmbi determine that the lands out yonder, swollen with fig trees and olive trees, those forests and mounts full of melodies—they will become home. But to reach Mũkũrũweinĩ—where swallows sing in the air, time flows like an endless river, pregnant clouds let down rain, and earth drinks the water to grow roots and bear fruits and flowers—Gĩkũyũ and Mũmbi must first overcome obstacles erected in their path by a malevolent nature.

Later, they will return to the same snow-capped mountaintop where the supreme giver put them, this time to ask for suitors for their daughters.

Leveraging the creation mythology of the Gĩkũyũ people, Ngũgĩ gives the story a credible beginning and makes the characters—teeming with life and purpose—matter. This supports the quest narrative's construction and encourages readerly immersion.

Worldbuilding through Culture

Csicsery-Ronay Jr. speaks of language as part of world-building in the physics and biologies of imaginary worlds. Language as culture is part of worldbuilding. Ngũgĩ uses the strong Gĩkũyũ slant of the novel, including the naming of people and places, as a core building block.

In speculative fiction, the works of Le Guin and Tolkien, for example, showcase elaborate worlds, crafted languages, and imaginative presentations that invite us to embrace what Richard Mathews terms "infinite possibility" in *Fantasy: The Liberation of Imagination* (2002). There is a large presence of language and sophistication in the fictional realms of Le Guin's Earthsea books and Tolkien's *The Lord of the Rings* (1954). Both authors love languages. In the Earthsea books, Le Guin establishes a power relation via the language of magic, the language of dragons, the language of nature, and the language of creation. For Tolkien the philologist, the culture and linguistics of Middle-earth are part of an investment in worldbuilding that manifests the iconic, literary status of his fantasy works.

Ngũgĩ shows intimate knowledge of his own world. He invests in an examination and comprehension of the Gĩkũyũ tradition, guiding his creation of a complex and believable imaginary world. It's a strange place, but under-standing its culture helps readers unfamiliar with it to see the realm of the Gĩkũyũ people with fresh eyes.

One wonders about the pitfalls of intricate, unusual names and places that emerge as obstacles. Card says to be careful about linguistic invention. "Can the human mouth pronounce it?" he asks. "Words or names that are mere collections of odd letters like *xxyqhhp* or *h'psps't* are doubly dumb, first because they constantly distract the reader and force him to withdraw from the story and think about the letters on the page, and second because even strange and difficult languages, when transliterated into the Roman alphabet, will follow Roman alphabetic conventions" (56). Ngũgĩ avoids these pitfalls because the Gĩkũyũ language is phonetically accessible, as are the names of the characters in *The Perfect Nine*. He calls attention to phonetics from the start in the prologue: "In Gĩkũyũ, the 'ũ' is pronounced like the 'o' in 'boat'; the 'ĩ' is pronounced like the 'a' in 'take' (ix).

In addition to language, Ngũgĩ invites us into the African world and its culture through place (thatched-roof huts, granaries full of harvest, kraals full of cows, goats, and sheep); through clothing (brides in soft leather skirts trimmed at the edge with multicolored beads, shells, necklaces, and copper rings around the women's necks); through food (goat meat, sweet potatoes, yams, arrowroots, millet, sorghum, herbal wine); through song and dance (drums, flutes, whistles, claps, ululations); and through the power of oral storytelling (as days came and went, feasting in daytime, storytelling in the evening) before embarking on the ultimate quest.

The Perfect Nine is deeply cultural, emphasizing the importance of naming in African tradition, the place of ceremony, and the heart of kinship bonded by blood or marriage. As one groom says to Gĩkũyũ and Mũmbi: "I want to talk to you, my father and my mother [...] For I cannot call you by any other name, given that you received me and accepted me as your son" (200). Through culture, Ngũgĩ builds on the basic concepts that run across the story, developing the history and rules of the invented world, then dramatizing them in a decidedly literary narrative that is not only accessible but fascinating.

Worldbuilding through Nature

There's good nature and bad nature. Mūmbi speaks of the power of the elements: "Water is life for humans, animals, and plants. Water makes the mud out of which life is molded. The sun sends rays of heat into the muddy dough, [a]nd breathes the breath of life into the dough. The earth drinks the water and seeds sprout" (188). Together with Gīkūyū and their daughters, she values the land of Mūkūrūweinī, its water, earth, air, and sun, the place where man, woman, birds, worms, animals, and creatures of the sea live as one with nature. Speaking to the suitors about the sacredness of land and nature, one daughter, Wambūi, says that "reverence for all life was one of the rules of Gīkūyū and Mūmbi. To harm plants and animals without good cause was to harm life. Never kill an animal unless in defense of self or to satisfy hunger. And if one uproots a tree, one must plant another to replace it" (69).

But not all nature is good. A hostile environment foreshadows a survivor's story, a narrative of courage, not only in Gīkūyū and Mūmbi, but in their daughters and suitors. A malevolent nature spews harms on the way, like the red boulders Gīkūyū and Mūmbi dodged, the ones that chased them to the plains before they reached Mūkūrūweinī; like the world that convulsed and erupted around them, ridges forming as the earth trembled, and tremors from the belly of the land forging valleys deep and wide; and like the rivers of fire, whose flames spurted skyward to devour hills and whose fumes incinerated the flora and fauna. There's darkness so deep, it makes the rest of the darkness look like day. It's a darkness shaped like a human, and echoes of sound herald the wandering of spirits in the forest.

And once Gĩkũyũ and Mũmbi cautiously deliver themselves to their home country, Mũkũrũweinĩ, their daughters and suitors will also face nature's harms in the shape of hurricanes that carried men in the air like leaves, wind that shuddered as it plummeted dying humans onto the land, rivers that refused to be clean but were murky with bamboo and crocodiles, grass that sank and swallowed men, not to mention the thorns, nettles, nests of red ants, dusts of tsetse flies, and otherworldly creatures hindering the journey. The power of nature allows Ngũgĩ to build and populate his invented world, breathing into it subversive messages of sustainability and humanity's (dis)harmony with the environment.

Worldbuilding through Otherworldly Creatures

Gĩkũyũ and Mũmbi, before they were safe in Mũkũrũweinĩ, encountered the dragon of the water that vomited white anger onto the shore. Now their daughters and suitors must contend with more otherworldly creatures in the darkness of forests that are pregnant with ogres.

One of these ogres is a king with magical hair on his tongue that can heal Warigia. But which suitor has the courage or cunning to retrieve the hair? Through the ogre of endless darkness, the ogre that fumes fire and fury, and the ogres that morph into a hyena and a vulture, we understand the hazardous landscape and the perils of the treasure hunt that endow more significance (and readerly gratification) to the story's climax and denouement.

And while beauty is in the eye of the beholder, we discover with Gĩkũyũ and Mũmbi's daughters and their suitors that there are inherently evil beauties:

Suddenly another wonder sprang up before us. I can't remember who first spotted him, but he was extremely well built, a beauty the color of chalk. The entire body, together with the clothes, was chalk white. His hair—long, straight, and soft-looking—fell on his back and shoulders. It was also chalky, whiter than the whiteness of an ostrich. But let the rays of the setting sun fall on his body and clothes, and they shone with more than the seven colors of the rainbow. And then he whistled at us. (163-64)

Another white beauty emerges, and she is equally ravishing. As the daughters and their suitors find distraction in the white, long-haired newcomers, Wanjikū comes to her senses and reprimands her siblings for preferring all that glitters. Just then, a strong wind blows and reveals the beauty for the skeleton it is—an ogre of the white chalk, wearing masks of human bodies and hair. And there's a moral to the story about coveting that which you don't know, about an exterior shell that conceals a raw interiority.

By his usage of otherworldly creatures in *The Perfect Nine*, Ngũgĩ successfully introduces vital tensions, inward turmoils, and outer conflicts that move the quest narrative forward and effectively bring it to a conclusion.

Coda

In *The Perfect Nine*, Ngũgĩ wa Thiong'o creates a nuanced literature of the strange, one that's accessible to readers because of its elaborate worldbuilding in the creation of culture, nature, and creatures. His own understanding of the Gĩkũyũ people, hosting the narration within the frameworks of Gĩkũyũ folklore and real-world traditions, helps to map an invented but relatable environment. The author's investment in worldbuilding compounds the credibility of his fiction to a universal reader in a work that piques curiosity in the mythologies and traditions of the Gĩkũyũ people as well as African literature in general.

References

Card, Orson Scott, *How to Write Science Fiction and Fantasy*. Writer's Digest Books, 1990.

Carver, Raymond. *A Storyteller's Shoptalk*. February 15, 1981. Online. Accessed May 30, 2020.

Csicsery-Ronay Jr., Istvan. "Who Framed Science Fiction." *Science Fiction Studies* 31.1 (March 2004): Online. Accessed May 30, 2020.

Gĩkũyũ Centre for Cultural Studies. *Gikuyu Origins*. 2020. Online. Accessed May 30, 2020.

Kariuki, Emmanuel. "Kikuyu, Meru, Gumba, and Chuka Myths of Origin." *Owlocation*. August 9, 2019. Online. Accessed May 30, 2020.

Mathews, Richard. *Fantasy: The Liberation of the Imagination*. Routledge, 2002.

Ngũgĩ wa Thiong'o. *Kenda Mũiyũru*. East African Educational Publishers Ltd., 2018.

———. *Petals of Blood*. Heinemann, 1977.

———. *The Black Hermit*. Makerere University Press, 1963.

———. *The Perfect Nine: The Epic of Gĩkũyũ and Mũmbi*. The New Press, 2020.

———. *The River Between*. Heinemann, 1965.

———. *Wizard of the Crow*. Harvill Secker, 2006.

Stockwell, Peter. *The Poetics of Science Fiction*. Longman, 2000.

Tolkien, J.R.R.. *The Lord of the Rings*. Allen & Unwin, 1954.

Vogler, Christopher. *The Writer's Journey*. Michael Wiese Productions, 1998.

AFRICAN CREATION MYTHS

Africa is large but highly diverse in geography, traditions, and linguistics. The continent bears a population of over 1.378 billion, an equivalent of 16.72 percent of the total world population ("African Population"). With such varied peoples and belief systems, African gods of creation are equally manifold and mostly male, summoned by a diversity of traditional names. Among them are Mungu (Swahili in Tanzania), Imana (Banyarwanda in Rwanda), Wele (Abaluyia in Kenya), Rugaba (Ankore in Uganda), Juok (Anuak and Shilluk in the Upper Nile), Kanu (Baga in Guinea), Ngai (Gĩkũyũ in Kenya), Nzame (Bantu of the Congo), Ruwa (Chagga in Tanzania), and Umvelinqangi (Xhosa in South Africa) ("African Mythology"). Other gods, likely also male, include Avrikit (the fisherman god), Amun (god of air and sun), Magec (god of sun and light), Zivelele (the self-existent one), Wele (god of creation), and Bukulu (god of the sky) ("All"). There are female gods, too, such as Edinkira (Ashanti people in Ghana), the goddess of healing and blessing; Mwambwa (Lozi people in Namibia), the goddess of lust and desire; and Achimi (Kabyle people in Algeria), daughter of the buffalo god Itherther ("African Mythology"). All traditional gods, in particular those of creation, play an important role in African ideologies, identities, and origin stories.

African creation stories have startling similarities. Consider the early migration of the Bantu people from southwest Africa to central, eastern, and southern parts of the continent about 5,000 years ago (Cartwright). The migration was typically a quest for food and fresh pastures or an escape from famine, epidemics, and warfare; in some cases, people simply wanted to go on an adventurous gallivant. It was inevitable that such migration would spread Bantu and Bantu-related languages, traditions, and mythologies (including creation stories) across the rest of Africa ("The Migration").

According to Elizabeth Prine Pauls, Bantu-speaking people comprise approximately 85 million of Africans, who exhibit distinct social, political, and cultural diversity, with elements of resemblance. Bantu speakers celebrate similar cultural rites of birth or coming of age, such as circumcision in men; in some Bantu groups (e.g., the Kisii people of Kenya) and Cushitic groups of the Afro-Asiatic family (e.g., the Iraqw in the Manyara regions of north-central Tanzania), it may be customary to practice female circumcision. There are also rites of marriage and death, which is not an *ending*, but a *passing* into another world. A key similarity among African peoples is patriarchal authority. Origin stories lean towards a male god who creates a "Great Man." This man, then, creates or discovers one or more wives, whose folly (like the biblical Eve's) might engender the death of humankind.

The sun, moon, and mountains in East Africa each play a central role in African folklore. Prominent mountains include the towering Mount Kirima Kĩrĩ Nyaga (the Gikuyu name for Mount Kenya), Mount Elgon, and Mount Kilimanjaro. Personified animals recur in the folklore, namely the tortoise, the hare, and the chameleon. The god of creation, Ruwa, of the Chagga people in Tanzania, conjured an Edenic garden atop Mount Kilimanjaro. Among the Maasai people in East Africa—who, incidentally, are not Bantu but Nilotic, a nomadic subgroup of the Nilo-Saharan family with its own language group and cultural practices—the dual-natured god Engai is a vengeful yet benevolent giver who bestows the first man with cattle as his birthright ("Maasai"). The Baganda share the cow's importance as a gift from their deity, the skygod Ggulu, to Kintu (first man) and Nnambi (first woman).

For the Fulani people (Mali), the god Doondari creates the first man from five elements: milk, iron, fire, water, and air. Man's own folly (without Woman) emerges in the face of his pride, which leads to punishments of blindness, sleep, worry, and ultimately death ("African Creation"). In a Congo origin myth, a god needs the moon's help to create the first man, Baatsi, out of clay. Aligned with the biblical story of Eve as the perpetrator, a pregnant woman eats the fruit of a forbidden Tahu tree. Where humankind once aged and returned to heaven, the god punishes them with mortality ("African Creation").

In an oral story by the Nyamwezi people in Tanzania, the creator is a man called Shida Matunda, whose name literally translates to "troubled fruits." Shida creates two women to be his wives. One day, his favorite wife dies. Shida buries her and waters her grave until she begins to sprout into a plant. During his absence, the jealous second wife hoes down the wife-plant. Devastated, Shida decrees that death will be the norm for all humans, animals, and plants.

In a Zulu origin story, god (or Umvelinqangi) dwells in his dark universe and bellows with thunder when he is enraged, making the world tremble with earthquakes. He creates a reed that proliferates into the swamp of Uthlanga. One day, a man grows from the end of a reed. This man's name is Unkulunkulu, and he is known as "the first ancestor" or "the Great One." More humans come out of the reed and Unkulunkulu determines that they shall be immortal. He sends a chameleon to foretell this message to humankind, but it's too slow. Unkulunkulu abandons the chameleon and sends a fast but forgetful lizard; it reaches its destination and proclaims that humans shall be mortal. As a result, humans start dying, and the chameleon changes color, mortified by its lethargy and failure to spare mankind from death (Baker).

The nature of the fast but forgetful messenger changes across African folklore from a lizard to a bird and, in some Kenyan cultures, even a dog, as with the Luyi tribe of the Zambezi ("Chapter II"). The origin from a reed perhaps explains a Lesotho custom of sticking a reed outside of a hut for a newborn child. Also in Tanzania is the story of a man who falls asleep on a reed from an island on Lake Victoria; he floats to a place called Musoma and founds the Wajita people. His genesis is unclear, but in keeping with the heteronormative, patriarchal essence of the folklore, somewhere along the line he creates or finds a woman.

A predominant cultural belief held by several African peoples is that the man is the head of his family. Such is the hierarchy that dictates how certain tribes in eastern and southern Africa (e.g., the Karamojong or Kalanga people) marginalize women so that, for instance, on her wedding night, a bride must sleep with her father-in-law, who validates her virginity ("Kalanga"). When a father dies, it is customary for his eldest son to take the family reins, superseding and sometimes commanding his own mother. For the Karamojong—and reportedly for the polygamous Kalanga culture—when a husband dies, his eldest son is expected to inherit the surviving wives. Sometimes a woman is married to a husband's brother ("Wife"). It's unclear if these practices emerge from patriarchal origin stories or if these origin stories produce African phallocentrism.

Notably, some tribes *do* have the female matriarch. Women play an important role among Kenya's Gĩkũyũ people, where the nine founding clans arise from the nine daughters of Gĩkũyũ (first man) and Mũmbi (first woman). In matriarchal clans, children belong to their mother. Sometimes this leads to severe cultural feuds in the event of a woman's intermarriage to a patriarchal tribe in which children belong to their father.

There *are* women goddesses like Edinkira (the Ashanti goddess in Ghana), a-Bol (the Baga goddess of Fertility in Guinea), Mboya (the Bantu mother goddess), and Abuk (the Dinka goddess of plants in Sudan) ("African Mythology"). There are also traditional queen mothers and prominent rulers in ancient Egypt—e.g., Neferneferuaten Nefertiti, Sobekneferu, and Cleopatra (Adhikari)—but they don't seem to be as rampant as their male counterparts in origin stories. In fact, one East African myth that features ruling women sees them treat men badly; in reaction, the men conspire to impregnate their female sovereigns and thereby overthrow them.

African folklore and origin myths possess inherent meaning and offer answers to important etymological questions of *how* and *why* things came to be. They were mostly orally told by elders to educate the young in a natural hierarchy of tradition and respect. Coupled with riddles, proverbs, sayings, music, and dance, stories were a valuable channel for social, cultural, and political education across generations as well as a critical device for community bonding and identity.

There are inevitable gaps in researching African origins stories today, and they are challenging to locate and verify. Colonial systems preferred to banish traditional cultural practices. Some traditions petered out with the infusion of Westernization and the encouragement of new languages, such as English in eastern parts of Africa (e.g., Kenya and Uganda), French in some central and western parts (e.g., the Congo and Senegal), and even Portuguese in some southern and western African countries (e.g., Angola and Guinea-Bissau). As more members of the older generations died without orally passing on their knowledge to the young, creation stories became lost or reformed.

Today African organizations and global centers for African studies, in collaboration with institutes of higher learning, continue to resurrect and make timeless these cultural artifacts (stories, riddles, proverbs, sayings, etc.) in living encyclopedias. But without voices from the "grassroots" (some of which no longer exist), and given the cross-cultural knowledge of the western-schooled researcher who might be less acquainted with the lived experience intrinsic to African mythology—is the resurrection authentic?

References

Adhikari, Saugat. "Top 9 Female Rulers of the Ancient World." *Ancient History Lists*. May 2, 2020. Online. Accessed August 20, 2021.

"African Creation Stories." *Exploring Africa*. n.d. Online. Accessed August 20, 2021.

"African Mythology: The Gods and Spirits of Africa." *Godchecker*. n.d. Online. Accessed August 20, 2021.

"Africa Population." *Worldometer*. n.d. Online. Accessed August 20, 2021.

"All the African God Names and Their Mythologies." *Kidadl.* n.d. Online. Accessed August 20, 2021.

Baker, David. "Origin Story: Zulu." *Khan Academy.* n.d. Online. Accessed August 20, 2021.

Cartwright, Mar. "Bantu Migration." *World History Encyclopedia.* April 11, 2019. Online. Accessed August 20, 2021.

"Chapter II: Where Man Came from, and How Death Came." *Sacred Texts.* n.d. Online. Accessed August 20, 2021.

"Kalanga: A Tribe/Culture Where the Bride Sleeps with her Father-in-Law on Wedding Night." *AWDesk.com.* September 25, 2019. Online. Accessed August 21, 2021.

"Kenya: Folklore." *East Africa Living Encyclopedia.* n.d. Online. Accessed August 20, 2021.

"Maasai Culture and History: Understanding the Soul of East Africa." *Zegrahm Expeditions.* January 29, 2018. Online. Accessed August 20, 2021.

Pauls, Elizabeth Prine. "Bantu Peoples." *Britannica.* January 19, 2007. Online. Accessed August 20, 2021.

"The Migration History of Bantu-Speaking People: Genomics Reveals the Benefits of Admixture and Sheds New Light on Slave Trade." *Institut Pasteur.* May 5, 2015. Online. Accessed August 20, 2021.

"Wife Inheritance: Karamoja Woman Married to Three Brothers." *NTV Uganda.* January 30, 2015. Online. Accessed August 20, 2021.

BECOMING VISIBLE
The Rise of Black Speculative Fiction

As an African Australian who has grappled with matters of identity, writing black speculative fiction is like coming out of the closet. It's a recognition that I'm Australian and African, and it's okay—the two are not mutually exclusive. I am many, I am *betwixt*, I am a sum of cultures. I am self and "other," a story of inhabitation, a multiple embodiment. And my multiplicities render themselves in cross-genre writing. As a reader, writer, and editor, I'm increasingly aware that black speculative fiction is on the rise.

It's not like black fiction was never there. I was always an avid reader from childhood, and my father rewarded my curiosity and good grades with African writing. I whet my tooth for literature on Margaret Ogola, Chinua Achebe, Camara Laye, and Ngũgĩ wa Thiong'o. Their writings are not always considered to be part of the speculative genre, but their novels introduced me to narratives with roots in traditional beliefs and oral literature. Growing up, I reveled in fairy tales featuring protagonists from the insect and animal world—the clever little monkey, the wise tortoise, and Ananse the spider—in "how" and "why" stories: how the frog came to be king of the rivers and marshes, how the tortoise got its scars, how the tortoise beat the hare in a race, why the bat flies at night, why the crab has no head ...

Years later, I became a member of the editorial team of *Aurealis*, Australia's premier speculative fiction magazine. Picture my delight when I stumbled across British-Nigerian Nuzo Onoh's African-hued "Ogali" (2019), an exemplar of black speculative fiction that's set in a small village and deploys the fantastical through black magic. The opening of the story immerses readers in Onoh's imagined world with a dreadful happening: "Ogali died on the dawn of her fifteenth birthday. She died gripping the wrist of the young man, Amobi, he of the roving eyes and honey-sweet tongue. Amobi swore he was not near her when she died, that he was with another virgin at a different village, engaged in the pleasures of the groin at the time of Ogali's death, just before dawn" (14).

Onoh creates tension while introducing dominant themes, characters, and the building blocks of this alternate world. We encounter the village, the tiny room that houses a young girl's corpse, and the center of the hamlet where a crowd gathers to witness black magic. The witchdoctor and his chanting urge the petrified young man to confess his crime: "Amobi, son of Obioha of Okoro clan, lift your shameless bottom from the floor and explain yourself to us before I curse you with the itchy pus-penis and eternal sterility, you disgraceful scoundrel" (16). Tension continues to build during the investigation of the alleged murder and Amobi's possible hand in it. The climax occurs when the corpse supernaturally draws attention to its killer.

The bizarreness of Ogali's sickness, the invoking of the occult, and the use of black magic and reanimation—these utilities incite a foreboding dread that sticks with (and to) us. Integrating fantasy, horror, and the paranormal, "Ogali" is also an example of fiction that effectively crosses genres.

Onoh is a pioneer of African horror and her work is published in several anthologies, notably *Dominion: An Anthology of Speculative Fiction from Africa and the African Diaspora* (2020), with stories in the subgenres of horror noir, Afrofuturism, sword and soul, steamfunk, and dieselfunk.

Another work of fiction that resonated with me is the young adult novel *Catching Teller Crow* (2018) by the Aboriginal Australian writers Ambelin Kwaymullina and Ezekiel Kwaymullina. I first came across it as a judge for the Aurealis Awards in 2020. It's an ingenious story told in shifting first-person perspectives by a brother and sister who come to grasp the tactic of stories-within-a-story as unreliable co-narrators. The novel borrows from the indigenous art of oration and adopts the levity of prose poetry and song, weaving together evocative imagery and personification in accessible language, and foregrounding themes of colonialism, survival, violence, selfhood, love, family, and identity. The Kwaymullinas speak to the plight of adolescents in particular, featuring a protagonist, Beth, who is the spirit of a dead girl, and a host of other characters in distress from whose perspectives we view the world.

Catching Teller Crow is more than just another story. It's a tale of courage, of remembering who you are. It takes a closer look at Australia's shameful past (i.e., the Stolen Generation) by exposing the strength of Nanna, a little black girl who found her way back home, years after the government took her away from her mother. At the same time, the novel is hopeful. The Kwaymullinas underscore the importance and strength of friendship; above all, they suggest that good friends can be transformative in numbers.

Near the end, Beth, her father Michael, and her newfound companions experience a full-circle transformation archetypal to the hero/ine story. As a cross-cultural narrative,

Catching Teller Crow charts new ground and stirs up deep anger, depression, and confusion before humming a tune of self-awakening and reflection.

This very personal novel is also universal despite its black protagonist. Unsurprisingly, it received several literary nominations and awards, winning the Victorian Premier YA Prize for Literature and the Best Young Adult Novel at the Aurealis Awards.

In a 1904 letter to Oskar Pollak, Franz Kafka wrote: "I think we ought to read only the kind of books that wound or stab us. If the book we're reading doesn't wake us up with a blow to the head, what are we reading for? [...] A book must be the axe for the frozen sea within us" (16). This was the axe that struck me when I read Namwali Serpell's debut novel *The Old Drift* (2019), which won the Art Seidenbaum Award and was a finalist for the inaugural Ray Bradbury Prize. It was also longlisted for the Center for Fiction's First Novel Prize. Speculative and literary, the novel grabbed me from the first line—"Zt. Ztt. ZZZzzz ... ZZZzzzzo'na" (1)—and commanded my attention until the end. It's a fantasy so subtle, it's extreme; a romance so fragile, it's lush; a political arena so subversive, it's sensational.

It's the language and the body of astonishments concealed in the rebellious, lengthy text that charmed me. Serpell explores ideology, supremacy, disease, and curiosity in relationships forged and lost. She casts a spotlight on the place of women in society, on the intolerable choices of mothers and their children, and on the quest for identity and belonging.

The Old Drift is Afrofuturistic in its gaze at colonization, independence, and regionalism. Serpell interrogates the challenges and intricacies of converging cultures through magical realism as well as speculative fiction, hurling upon its gullible cast the cruelty of fate sprinkled with impish humor, even in secondary characters like the Lusaka housemaid Grace, who calls bedsheets *shittybeds* in the thinness of her borrowed language. The novel is thoroughly researched, too—a fiction of fictions, a poignant grandiosity lavish in language and intimate with Africa, where entire histories of pent-up resentment finally bellow in rage.

Serpell is a Zambian writer and professor at the University of California-Berkeley. She received a Rona Jaffe Foundation Writers' Award for female authors in 2011, and she was selected for the Africa 39, a 2014 Hay Festival project to identify the best African writers under 40. Her first published story, "Muzungu," which means "white man" in Swahili, was selected for *The Best American Short Stories 2009* and shortlisted for the 2010 Caine Prize for African writing. She won the Caine Prize for her story "The Sack" in 2015.

Another book I love is Wole Talabi's bold, experimental *Incomplete Solutions* (2019). Reading this fiction collection took me back to Nobel Laureate Toni Morrison and Roland Barthes' playfulness with language. As Barthes contends in *The Pleasure of the Text* (1973), fiction is a figment of our imagination, and text is a tissue of quotations arising from thousands of cultural sources from which both writers and readers extrapolate meaning. Talabi encourages this extrapolation in stories that are sharp, brisk, and metafictional, with insightful narrators who haul us into weird but captivating worlds.

Talabi is not your typical short-story writer. He takes readers on a strange, transcultural odyssey that's filled with Yoruba mythology, nested logic, and recurring themes of the unknown, variability, equation, relationship, sacrifice, betrayal, transposition, escapade … His fiction subverts our expectations. We find gods and goddesses, victims and victors, alternate beings or "alters" who exist in realms of virtual reality and cyber-consciousness. Each of Talabi's stories pose questions or curiosities with a sensitivity and perception that sticks with me to this day.

What I realize in these readings (and much black speculative fiction) is the vital conversation about blackness itself.

I remember the last of my writerly engagements early in 2020 before COVID restrictions. There was a cascade of event cancellations. Writing NSW in Australia invited me to participate in an all-black panel on Africa for its Talking Writing series. Curated and chaired by the actor, writer, and activist Moreblessing Maturure, and funded by the Copyright Agency Cultural Fund, our conversation gave voice to the hierarchies of blackness in Australia and cast its gaze on the complex, diverse experiences of African migrants and Afro descendant peoples relative to indigenous peoples. After the panel, participants from ethnic minority groups—some with Lebanese, Israeli, and Cambodian heritage—shared how insightful it was to find writing that featured an "other" because they were always trying to "fit in."

Speculative fiction invites authors to bend genres and encourages them to deconstruct normative conventions in experimental, adventurous ways. I'm thrilled that more black writers are (re)inventing the idea of self, becoming more outspoken, and syphoning creative and intellectual energy from the ever-expanding monster of culture. Irrespective of race, readers and publishers are increasingly fascinated by black speculative fiction, and there are even exclusive awards (e.g., the Nommo Award) that recognize works by Africans and are judged by African writers (e.g., from the African Speculative Fiction Society).

The novels and stories I have shared in earnest with you in this article are exemplars of diverse black fiction. With a growing openness by publishers to look at different kinds

of narratives and attract black writing, there is an unques-
tionable rise of black speculative fiction in the market.
It's a valuable, important thing for people of color who
are looking for stories that feature relatable "others" like
them. I discuss this in my essay collaboration with African
American author Milton J. Davis, "The State of Black Speculative Fiction," which appears in *Hadithi and the State of
Black Speculative Fiction* (2020). In the essay, Davis and I
open up a dialogue about Afrofuturism, speculative fiction,
and genre-crossing by black writers. The abstract reads:

> As speculative fiction authors are increasingly curious
> and experimental in a competitive publishing industry,
> crossing genres to subvert readers' expectations, writers
> of color are ever more claiming their right to tell their
> own stories in invented worlds with characters they can
> identify with. This new brand of writing is taking form
> in small-press Afrofuturistic dystopias, myths and epics
> delivered to a growing readership that is open-minded
> and inquisitive. But, until black speculative fiction is
> normalized, there's still a long way to go. (1)

We need more publishers to step up and encourage
writing that gives voice to minority ethnic groups. Black
speculative fiction is out there—you only have to seek it
out. We also need a growing readership that is curious and
welcoming to this new brand of Afrocentric writing by
authors whose texts are a sum of cultures—or, as Deleuze
and Guattari might say, whose texts are "*intermezzo*" (25).
Until more readers, publishers, agents, and literary-award
judges start paying attention to stories of inhabitation,
multiple embodiments, and inclusivity across cultures, the
rise of this caliber of fiction will linger in the margins.

References

Bacon, Eugen and Davis Milton. *Hadithi and the State of Black Speculative Fiction*. Luna Press Publishing, 2020.

Barthes, Roland. *The Pleasure of the Text*. Trans. Richard Miller. Hill and Wang, 1973.

Deleuze, Gilles and Fèlix Guattari. *A Thousand Plateaus*. 1980. Trans. Brian Massumi. University of Minnesota Press, 1987.

Kafka, Franz. *Letters to Friends, Family, and Editors*. Trans. Richard Winston. Schocken, 1990.

Knight, Zelda and Donald, Ekpeki Oghenechovye. *Dominion: An Anthology of Speculative Fiction from Africa and the African Diaspora*. Aurelia Leo, 2020.

Kwaymullina, Ambelin and Kwaymullina Ezekiel. *Catching Teller Crow*. Allen and Unwin, 2018.

Onoh, Nuzo. "Ogali." *Aurealis* 118 (March 2018): 13-24.

Serpell, Namwali. *The Old Drift*. Hogarth, 2019.

Talabi, Wole 2019. *Incomplete Solutions*. Luna Press Publishing, 2019.

I WENT LOOKING FOR AFROSF

It was a love and hate relationship with M.

Occasionally, the brusque nature of my editorial colleague came across as pomposity and I told him what I thought of him. But that didn't stop M. from asking me for an occasional favor.

"How about a pitch?" he once asked me. "I've seen this AfroSF thing on Amazon a couple of times. It would be great to write an article."

M. was offering an olive branch. He wanted me to write something for his magazine. And I had just the title: "What Is AfroSF?"

It was a journey of discovery that led me to a new community. At the time, I didn't know much about AfroSF. I anticipated a deviant from SF's many subgenres and categories, and of course it had something to do with Africa.

An online search steered me to a 406-paged anthology published in 2012 by StoryTime, an African micropress dedicated to publishing short fiction by emerging and established African writers. Formed in 2007, StoryTime aspired to fill a lack in the African literary scene.

Some readers described the anthology as a groundbreaking work of diversity and hope, an "African Genesis" that was intense, varied, and fresh. In it, publisher and editor Ivor W. Hartmann spoke of his dream for an original, innovative anthology of SF by African authors called *AfroSF*. His vision was clear: "SciFi is the only genre that enables African writers to envision a future from *our* African perspective."

I admired this Zimbabwean writer, editor, publisher, and visual artist. In particular, I was impressed with *Mr. Goop*, his award-winning, postapocalyptic novelette about a boy who struggles with coming-of-age concerns like bullies and scholarly performance in a science-fiction society called the United States of Africa, which is guarded by robots and chaperoned by humanoid genoforms.

Like most anthologies, *AfroSF* showcased great as well as ordinary stories, some by first-timers having a crack at publication, others by established award-winners like Nnedi Okorafor and her contribution, "Moom!," a modern fable about a swordfish attack on the oil industry. Additional standouts include Biram Mboob's "The Rare Earth," a dark tale of pilgrimage, exploitation, and annihilation in the Congo, where there exists a black messiah in a male-dominated world; Liam Kruger's "Closing Time," a cynical monologue of booze-driven time travel; Joan De La Haye's "The Trial," set in a futuristic world of human culling that targets prisoners, old people, artists, and writers, poignantly told from the perspective of a fated author; and Chinelo Onwualu's "The Gift of Touch," a space odyssey with African passengers and a backstory of priests, human sacrifice, and a gift of healing.

A commonality in the anthology involved an element of "culture" in worlds abounding with African characters, suns, and horizons. The stories embraced a wealth of SF tropes: teleporting, futuristic worlds in African landscapes, artificial intelligence, iris scanners, data mining, body irrigation, child regeneration, cyberpunk, space opera, aliens … It also addressed themes prevalent in the African continent, such as war, crime, poverty, and HIV.

Later, I looked up some books and came across Camara Laye's *The Radiance of the King* (1971). I wondered if it captured the essence of AfroSF, too. In this novel, a white man, Clarence, shipwrecked on the coast of Africa, longs to see the king that sold him to a harem as a sex slave. At the end of Clarence's disturbing exile is a revelation about his own humanity in the magnificence of the king. I pondered how effectively philosophical, existential, and postcolonial themes came together to align the novel with soft SF. For instance, it was comparable to the science-versus-religion motif in Ray Bradbury's "The Man" (1951). But nobody was promoting Laye's book as AfroSF. In fact, it was selling hotly as a literary classic and an epic African expression of the colonial period. In a review for *The New York Times*, Martin Tucker called it "allegorical, Kafkaesque and African in a unique way." "AfroSF" was not a term connected to it.

As my search continued, I stumbled across the African Speculative Fiction Society (ASFS), whose membership included writers, editors, graphic artists, and filmmakers in the fields of speculative fiction, and whose stories drew on tradition, philosophy, and science. To become a member, one had to meet certain criteria. Here is what the ASFS membership page said:

> We have a welcoming and inclusive definition of who is African. The term African includes: citizens of African countries, people born on the continent and raised there for substantial periods of time, citizens or people born on the continent who live abroad, people who have at

least one African parent, Africans without papers, and some migrants to African countries. ("Who")

A footnote further indicated: "'African country' is defined as any country or contested area on the Continent of Africa, ending at the Egyptian border, and including islands such as Zanzibar and Madagascar" (ibid.).

Notably, the society administered the Nommo Awards, which, according to the ASFS website, is "an African SF prize for Africans by Africans that honors our stories and how we choose to tell them" ("About Nommos"). Eligible entries to the Nommos were by authors who met the society's definition of an African.

Realizing that a swath of ASFS members contributed works in the original pan-African anthology *AfroSF*, I scanned the society's website to see if members regarded their individual creative artifacts outside the anthology as AfroSF. They did not. The website bore no mention, definition of, or identification with AfroSF.

Around that time, the tri-monthly magazine *Omenana* came up in online search results. Co-founded by Chinelo Onwualu, whose "The Gift of Touch" appeared in *AfroSF*, this prominent, English-language, speculative-fiction periodical accepted submissions of art, fiction, and nonfiction by artists and writers from Africa and the African Diaspora. It demonstrated a close affiliation with the ASFS by guiding its readers to the society's definition of who is an African. In the submission guidelines, *Omenana* classified "speculative" as fantasy, SF, horror, or magical realism, and the editors required characters, settings, or themes directly related to the African continent. Once again, I checked to see if any of the works published in the magazine were labelled AfroSF. Nothing.

With this knowledge, I wrote an article called "What is AfroSF?" I deduced that, while there existed African-themed, African-cast, and African-set SF, fantasy, and horror, AfroSF was neither a literary movement nor a subgenre of SF. It was a series of anthologies. Period. The term solely referred to the specific anthology (and its sequels) of SF by writers or African heritage. Nobody was calling anything else AfroSF.

But I gained something from the hunt. I became a member of the African Speculative Fiction Society and developed an affiliation with this community. My curiosity was ultimately rewarded by my discovery of black speculative fiction and especially Afrofuturism.

Since the term's creation in the 90s by Mark Dery, scholarly essays on Afrofuturism have increasingly reimagined the past and present experiences of the African diaspora, exploring what black futures could look like. The African diaspora—as in the ASFS definition—refers to people whose ancestors migrated from the continent, were snatched from it, or were still there, and it included anyone of African descent in Europe, North America, South America, Asia, the Antarcticas, Australia, Oceania, and Africa itself. Unified by a shared heritage, each had their unique languages, cultures, and stories that diversified their critical articulations of a reimagined Africa.

Today, Afrofuturism has expanded its outlook beyond literature and music to the visual arts, religion, and even philosophy in an ongoing extrapolation of possibilities and probabilities. There are problems with definitions, and some will insist on distinctions between Afrofuturism and Africanfuturism, or other terms associated with black speculative fiction. In *Paratexts: Thresholds of Interpretation* (1997), French literary theorist Gérard Genette explores the liminal devices and conventions that form a complex mediation between a book and its author, publisher, and readers. Where titles, forewords, epigraphs, and the publisher's jacket can help endow a work's significance as part of its private and public history, however, once readers engage with it from their own unique perspectives, the work is unchained from its origin. Readers deconstruct the text and assign their own subjective interpretations.

Contemporary writers like Nisi Shawl continue to think that work about the black experience that is at the center of the speculative universe is Afrofuturistic. In a 2019 lecture on Afrofuturism, Shawl says black figures like director Ryan Coogler, author Octavia Butler, and singer-songwriter Janelle Monáe have one thing in common: they create decidedly Afrofuturistic artifacts. The lecture celebrated past, present, and future Black Americans vis-à-vis their important contributions to art, literature, science, music, film, and more. Here and elsewhere, Shawl's voice is important, if not vital. In "Everfair: Afrofuturist Alternate History," a 2018 paper originally presented at the Worlding SF conference in Graz, Austria, Sean Guynes contends that Shawl's novel *Everfair* (2016) is a conceptual space for thinking about Afrofuturism's relation to history, temporality, and the political present, drawing upon the relationship between the narrative indexes of Afrofuturism, alternate history, and history itself.

I'm drawn to these words from P. Djèlí Clark's "How to Spite a Racist Troll: Support Black Dreams": "One of the ways speculative fiction can work against racism and [colonization] is to reimagine our past, altering the power dynamics that we are accustomed to in order to illuminate hidden histories and silenced voices."

In the end, M.'s unusual request (and my subsequent research) changed our relationship—he was genuinely interested in black writing. It turns out M. wasn't that much of an alpha-dick after all. Setting me on the hunt for a feature article to define AfroSF was a gift. Suddenly, I was unblinkered and began to easily spot black people's stories of social movement, technology, artistic expression, critical embodiment, postmodernism, and other cultural effusions.

Thereafter, M. loved the ideas I pitched to him for publication. We found common ground in a variety of material, such as cyberfunk (distinguished by the transformative effects of information technology), sword and soul (rooted in sorcery and "black" magic), blacktastic (fantastical adventures where black hero/ines find reward), steamfunk (like steampunk, based on Victorian machinery), dieselfunk (the Jazz Age meets SF), black-tech (present-day or alternate-reality technological "intrapolations"), rococoa (alternate history set against the backdrop of slavery or piracy), blaxploitation (primarily films that ab/use black stereotypes and superhero/ines), and black horror (specific to that which might frighten diasporic peoples).

Hartmann's follow-ups to *AfroSF*, *AfroSF v2* (2015) and *AfroSF v3* (2018), further encapsulate these subgenres. I just might write a story for yet another multicultural anthology, this one with a call for futuristic submissions on the state of Earth and the theme of climate crisis. M., you're welcome.

References

"About Nommos." *African Speculative Fiction Society*. n.d. Online. Accessed October 14, 2021.

Bacon, Eugen. "What is AfroSF?" *Aurealis* 111 (June 2019): 41-47.

Clark, P. Djèlí "How to Spite a Racist Troll: Support Black Dreams." *The Musings of a Disgruntled Haradrim*. April 11, 2015. Online. Accessed May 24, 2020.

Gennette, Gérard. *Paratexts: Thresholds of Interpretation.* Cambridge University Press, 1997.

Guynes, Sean. "Everfair: Afrofuturist Alternate History." *Seanguynes.com.* December 1, 2019. Online. Accessed May 24, 2020.

Hartmann, Ivor W., ed. *AfroSF: Science Fiction by African Writers.* StoryTime, 2012.

Laye, Camara. *The Radiance of the King.* Collier Books, 1971.

Shawl, Nisi. "Afrofuturism 101 with Nisi Shawl." *The Stranger.* February 10, 2019. Online. Accessed May 24, 2020.

Tucker, Martin. "Son of the Buffalo Painter." *The New York Times.* June 24, 1984. Online. Accessed October 14, 2021.

"Who Is African?" *African Speculative Fiction Society.* n.d. Online. Accessed October 14, 2021.

AFROFUTURISM
A WorldCon Recap, and Some Thoughts

Afrofuturism was an important topic at the virtual 2020 WorldCon in New Zealand. In panel discussions, the term generally applied to literary works that use the frame of SF, fantasy, or horror to reimagine the past and present experiences of the African diaspora and to explore the potential contours of a black futurology.

In addition to me, there were four people on the panel: Suyi Davies Okungbowa, a renowned Nigerian author of fantasy, SF, and horror inspired by his West-African origins; Brandon O'Brien, a writer, performance poet, game designer, and then-editor of *Fiyah Magazine* from Trinidad and Tobago; Ekpeki Oghenechovwe, a Nigerian writer who had won a Nommo Award for Best Story and received two honorable mentions from the L. Ron Hubbard Writers of the Future Contest; and Maquel A. Jacob, a multi-generic author and the owner of MAJart Works. Jacob moderated the panel and skillfully facilitated discussion among the panelists while fielding questions from the audience.

Here's the panel description that appeared on the convention program:

According to *Yes! Magazine*, the concept of Afrofuturism may only go back to 1966, when the Black Panther first appeared in a Marvel comic and Lt. Uhura first appeared on Star Trek. The recent MCU movie, *Black Panther*, shone a bright light onto this subgenre. Our panel explores its origins, what it encompasses, and what works they recommend for getting more familiar with the subgenre. ("On Afrofuturism")

From the beginning, I was enthralled with what would become a hearty dialogue between my fellow panelists about the divergent views of Afrofuturism.

Okungbowa did not believe what he wrote was Afrofuturism. He agreed that the term considered the possibilities existent in a person of African descent living anywhere in the future. But blackness, he said, exists in various ways across the globe and it's impossible to flatten into a single term; "Afrofuturism" is a projection of what blackness means today and what blackness might mean in the future.

O'Brien suggested that acceptance or understanding of the term depended on one's relationship with the world. He found it problematic to attach a single word "given to us by a white man" to the diaspora. For him, Afrofuturism was a potential silo of black futuristic imagination, a way of seeing the value of *known works*, rather than a means of finding lesser-known works that may not thrive in a prefigured space or fit the lens that the publishing and film industries had already applied to the term. It would be interesting, he said, to see what the literary and cinematic elite planned to do with the term. Would they uplift or bludgeon the creative output of black people?

Oghenechovwe saw limitations in the "us" (black people) within the "afro" where the reach of the term was not clearly defined or satisfactory, especially if it pertained to the broader diaspora and the *exclusion* of stories from within the African continent itself. He reminded the audience to be aware that there already existed lesser-known works by writers and publishers like Milton Davis and Balogun Ojetade (who coined the term dieselfunk).

Other writers and scholars have devised alternative terms.

Afropolitan has been used for diasporic African fiction written by authors like Taiye Selasi, Yvonne Owuor, Sefi Atta, Chimamanda Ngozi Adichie, Nalo Hopkinson, and Teju Cole. The term went viral after the publication of Selasi's essay "Bye-Bye Babar" in *LIP Magazine* in 2005; she uses it to define African artists with global and multicultural sensibilities. Afropolitan also extends to music, dance, food, and fashion. According to Brendah Nyakudya, "An Afropolitan is someone who has roots in Africa, raised by the world, but still has an interest in the continent and is making an impact, is feeding back into the continent and trying to better it" (Tutton).

Ethno-gothic was coined by professor, author, and illustrator John Jennings to denote a subgenre of the fantastic depicting the black experience in the speculative arts. It includes the black superhero and is aligned with Blacktastic—fantastical adventures featuring black hero/ines. In a recap of a book club discussion about Octavia Butler's *Kindred* (1979), Sherese Francis says that ethno-gothic texts exhibit "several elements: doppelgängers (double consciousness, the shadow taking shape, what happens when the shadow gets agency), anti-heroes, false histories, the black body as grotesque, tensions with the past, present and future, magic and the supernatural, and torture and abuse of the body."

Africanfuturism, Nnedi Okorafor explains, "is similar to 'Afrofuturism' in the way that blacks on the continent and in the Black Diaspora are all connected by blood, spirit, history and future. The difference is that Africanfuturism is specifically and more directly rooted in African culture, history, mythology and point-of-view as it then branches into the Black Diaspora, and it does not privilege or center the West."

These are three of numerous alternative terms. Rather than get hung up on definitions, however, perhaps what's more important to us black writers is that we leverage our valuable storytelling space in order to reckon with our histories and reveal the possibilities in social justice, healthcare, security, technology ... Above all, Okungbowa suggested in the panel discussion, we must tell stories that give answers to questions about how we can be better, how we can be more, how we can grow.

In my view, there was no need for dichotomy. All terms led to black-people stories in speculative fiction and embodied the prospect of manifesting a new kind of storytelling.

The panel reached a consensus that the movie *Black Panther* (2018)—despite its universally enthusiastic reception by black people—is not an accurate representation of Afrocentric cultures. As O'Brien clearly said (to the laughter of the panelists), a lot in the film is not only untrue for some diasporic communities, it is *definitively false.*

What *Black Panther* did do positively, suggested Oghenechovwe, was "make people look." Suddenly, the world became curious about black-people stories, about futuristic SF with elements of African culture.

The panel also took a collective position regarding the appropriation or misappropriation of African cultures by authors of non-African descent, as seen in texts like Neil Gaiman's *Anansi Boys* (2005), which depicts an incarnation of the West African trickster god Anansi. Anansi stories had long been told by black people from Ghana. What made Gaiman, a white person in a position of privilege with access to publishers, the right person to tell this story? Did Gaiman's trickster have to be Anansi? Would the commercialization and visibility of *Anansi Boys* above those intrinsic narratives by black people be a risk insofar as readers might perceive Gaiman's character to be the most accurate representation of the West African god?

After WorldCon, I reflected on the important conversations I'd had with my esteemed colleagues about Afrofuturism and similar formations. Below are some notes.

Afrofuturism: Scope

In the context of Mark Dery's introduction of Afrofuturism in "Black to the Future: Interviews with Samuel R. Delany, Greg Tate, and Tricia Rose" (1994), the term historically pertained to African-American experience and the black diaspora. Since then, it has grown in scope to embrace art, literature, music, style, etc. from within the African continent and its diaspora.

The African diaspora includes people who are citizens of African countries, people born on the continent and raised there for substantial periods of time, citizens of people born on the continent who live abroad, people who have at least one African parent, Africans without papers, and some migrants to African countries (i.e., countries within the continent and islands such as Zanzibar and Madagascar).

In a wider sense, Afrofuturism is inclusive of those whose ancestors migrated or were taken from the continent and anyone of African descent in Europe, North America, South America, Asia, Antarctica, Australia, Oceania, and Africa itself. Unified by a shared heritage, each has its own unique languages, cultures, and stories that render diversity to their critical imaginations of a reimagined Africa.

If Afrofuturism is to reimagine Africa in all its diversity, to expand and extrapolate it through literature, music, the visual arts, religion, even philosophy … how is this limiting?

The problem, as Oghenechovwe pointed out, arises when stories from within the African continent are excluded from Afrofuturism by critics, academia, or the industry, motivating some creators (e.g., Okungbowa and Oghenechovwe himself) to exclude their works from the term's coverage.

Afrofuturism: Genesis

A white man coined the term Afrofuturism. Think about it.

Dery did not create the term "afro." Remember the Commodores? Boney M.? Those bands flourished in the 70s. Remember the hair? That's an *afro*. Dictionary definitions typically refer to it as a long, bushy hairstyle sometimes worn by people of the African diaspora.

There's another definition, though. Afro is a form, a meaning—"of African."

You may be familiar with moments in history—namely in the 1930s, 40s, and 50s—bearing themes of black power as a literary and artistic movement among black thinkers and artists. For example, among French-speaking African and Caribbean writers living in Paris, the movement was a protest against French colonial rule and the policy of assimilation (i.e., French Négritude). Afro poetry and afro rhythms (e.g., Bob Marley) were also a thing. That was long before the 90s and Dery's article.

As with afro, Dery didn't create the term "futurism" either. Futurism originated as an early-twentieth-century Italian artistic movement whose texts emphasized speed, technology, and violence, led by charismatic poet Filippo Marinetti ("Futurism"). In effect, then, Dery helped himself to two terms already in use, each with its own inherent meaning, then married them into a portmanteau that synthesized those meanings.

There are many avenues of black-people narratives about social movement, technology, artistic expression, critical embodiment, and postmodernism that are bound to the marriage of "afro" and "futurism."

We can write about Africa, see it in a new light, tell stories of diversity and hope, stories of social justice, possibilities, probabilities, engaging with difference, dealing with the "other," hybridity, queering, origin tales about finding out who you are …

We can fight for freedom from discernible and concealed chains in different kinds of Afrofuturistic writings, as Octavia Butler did so effectively in her works on the black experience.

Black writers will determine the semantics of Afrofuturism. The stories we tell will represent that determination.

There's wealth in the diversity of our voices—we can sway power dynamics, illuminate hidden histories, give voice to those who cannot speak from the margins.

Other "Futurisms"

At WorldCon NZ, I gained an important insight into other "futurisms."

One panel moderated by Ian Nichols as part of the academic program covered ethnicities and perspectives on speculative fiction. I presented a joint paper with Milton Davis on the state of black speculative fiction. A revision of the paper was eventually published as a formal essay in the collection *Hadithi and the State of Black Speculative Fiction* (2020).

My colleague Gina Cole presented a paper titled "Wayfinding Pasifikafuturism: An Indigenous Science Fiction Vision of the Ocean in Space." For Cole, Pasifikafuturism is a theoretical construct inspired by Afrofuturism (and its Indigenous Futurisms kin) that situates Māori and Pasifika SF in the afterlife of colonization.

This sparked my curiosity about futurisms ...

Pasifikafuturism, in Cole's view, marks the intersection of multiple diasporas of Indigenous Pacific peoples who envision, dream, imagine, create, or are receptive to ideas that play with and liquify the boundaries of technology, time, and space. To make her case, she cited examples from Grace Dillon's *Walking the Clouds* (2012), Albert Wendt's *Black Rainbow* (1995), Chris Baker's *Kokopu Dreams* (2000), and Ambelin Kwaymullina's *The Interrogation of Ashala Wolf* (2013).

Amazofuturism concerns Brazilian Indigenous Futurism and has primarily manifested as artwork (e.g., the illustrations of J. Queiroz). Vítor Castelões Gama and Marcelo

Velloso Garcia say this SF subgenre represents the Amazon region "in a more positive light, often with an aesthetic akin to cyberpunk and solarpunk."

Arabfuturism is a reaction to Euro-American xenophobia and racism as discussed in Perwana Nazif's 2018 essay "Arabfuturism: Science-Fiction & Alternate Realities in the Arab World." A sentiment more than a literary movement, it borrows from Afrofuturism in its expanse across film, music, literature, and other media in a Pan-Arabist context; it's also an expression of self and collective identity. Arabfuturism is closely linked to **Gulf Futurism**. Coined by Qatari-American author Sophia Al-Maria and Kuwaiti musician Fatima Al Qadri, "the term suggests that certain aspects of how the West imagines the future are already manifest in the Gulf states of the Middle East," denoting architecture, art, urban planning, and popular culture in a cross-cultural alliance (Balsom).

In a Nutshell ...

Terms and definitions may be fads or here to stay. Surely more effects will result from the cause of "Afrofuturism" (e.g., **Sinofuturism**, a radical technological vision of futuristic China as simulated in artist Lawrence Lek's video-essay "Sinofuturism 1838-2046 A.D."). Whichever iteration of futurism an author, artist, or scholar brings to bear, the term should not be flat or monolithic. It should be pregnant with possibility—the galaxy is our oyster.

References

Balsom, Erika. "Sophia Al-Maria on Dystopias, Gulf Futurism, and Sad Sacks." *Art in America*. April 7, 2020. Online.

Accessed October 23, 2021.

Francis, Sherese. "Cosmic Ghost at the Museum: Notes from Kindred Book Club." *Futuristically Ancient.* November 26, 2013. Online. Accessed October 20, 2021.

"Futurism." *TheArtStory.org.* n.d. Online. Accessed February 13, 2022.

Gama, Vítor Castelões and Marcelo Velloso Garcia. "Amazofuturism and Indigenous Futurism in Brazilian Science Fiction." *Vector.* September 4, 2020. Online. Accessed October 23, 2021.

Nazif, Perwana. "Arabfuturism: Science-Fiction & Alternate Realities in the Arab World." *The Quietus.* February 22, 2018. Online. Accessed August 12, 2020.

Okorafor, Nnedi. "Africanfuturism Defined." *Nnedi Wahala's Zone.* October 19, 2019. Online. Accessed October 20, 2021.

"On Afrofuturism." *CoNZealand 2020.* July 30, 2020. Online. Accessed October 26, 2021.

Tutton, Mark. "Young, Urban and Culturally Savvy, Meet the Afropolitans." *CNN.com.* February 17, 2012. Online. Accessed October 19. 2021.

ON SLIPSTREAM
A Personal View

There's no manual on slipstream fiction. Think of it as fiction that abandons genre. The term "slipstream" was seemingly devised in 1989 by renowned American cyberpunk author Bruce Sterling for obscure stories that are neither mainstream nor genre SF. In *The Encyclopedia of Science Fiction*, John Clute says slipstream SF was devised "in part as a pun on, or echo of, Mainstream [...] to designate stories which make use of SF devices but which are not genre SF."

Jorge Luis Borges, one of Latin America's most influential writers, is a slipstream master whose irrealist, existential stories metafictionally deconstruct meaning and (in)validate purpose. *Labyrinths* (1962), a collection of irreal parables and essays, is probably his most-read book. In the meta-essay "Borges and I," the author interrogates the self:

> The other one, the one called Borges, is the one things happen to. I walk through the streets of Buenos Aires and stop for a moment, perhaps mechanically now, to look at the arch of an entrance hall and the grillwork on the gate; I know of Borges from the mail and see his name on a list of professors or in a biographical dictionary. I

like hourglasses, maps, eighteenth-century typography, the taste of coffee and the prose of Stevenson; he shares these preferences, but in a vain way that turns them into the attributes of an actor. (211)

Borges' characters and fictions chronically flirt with autobiography. They are projections of his self: the writer, the reader, the human being, the dreamer who is the dreamed one, the detective who deceives himself, the mirror portraying itself. While his work is best categorized as irreal—see G.S. Evans and Alice Wittenburg's *The Irreal Reader* (2013)—with Gabriel Garcia Márquez, Borges has also been called a father of magic realism, the tropes of which share common ground with slipstream fiction and are to some degree interchangeable, absorbing other genres and knowingly mutating them.

It's impossible for me to talk about slipstream fiction without mentioning European author Andrew Hook, who I interviewed for *Aurealis*. Hook excites me in an almost erotic way. His writing thrums and throbs in my head; it's full of pleasures and despairs. It's an organic writing—he feels it, gives every inch of himself in a single moment of intercourse. Well, let's call it immersion.

Hook's stories are decidedly weird, yet they speak to the human condition. He writes about coincidences without consequences. And he writes from the heart, the gut. His texts seem to shape themselves, unafraid of the perception of others. There's no three-act structure or hero/ine's journey—none of those hackneyed fictional conventions or devices. Sometimes there's not even a beginning, middle, or end; the end might be the middle, or vice versa. It doesn't matter. The plot is not the integral drive. Hook *hooks* readers with a voice that is at once unique, raw, emotional, and deviant.

This approach works best for experimental writers who might be curious about strange and innovative literary techniques. I ended up co-authoring a short story with Hook. I couldn't help it; working with him was like the enchantment of adultery, and I came to understand his method with greater clarity.

The story we wrote, "Messier 94," is a process of mind, a way of being at a point in time. I have worked with other authors before, but nothing fulfilled me like this collaboration. The rhythm of our writing filled me with anticipation and a magnificent tension. Pulse, texture—only the moment mattered. The mathematics of our words were sensual, spiritual, fantastical. And it bled into the writing itself:

> I looked at me, studying me with coldness or curiosity across blinking glass. Fraternal twins, identical but shifting sex. Everything was fleeting, voiceless, like an online story, an alien invasion—appearing everywhere into the suburbs, slowly around the city, where the numbers were okay but it was all mechanical.
>
> The mirror was a language in collapsing time, memos on an Earth overgrown with weeds, a random spread of flowers. Each new study of myself was a pulse ticking with tales full of questions, each a one-night fling that begot someone else's child. (84)

And later:

> Suddenly he grabbed my elbow. He was there, dancing with me. He was here, he was there—his fresh young face, eyes lit with mischief. We were tight. We were tense. We were fluid. Assembling, reassembling. She was back, she was forth—dark sweet notes of her perfume,

blue-black hair in a fringe across her face. They were handsome. They were dangerous. I was playing a game, and it was deadly. (100)

In my interview, I asked Hook: "You're a parent. How does a parent write a nasty yet enticing collection like *The Forest of Dead Children*?" Hook replied: "Precisely because I have children. As a parent, I'm torn between the joy of having them and the regret of having them. I think acknowledging that children are equally a burden as they are a bonus is important, but you don't often hear that honesty. Children change your life irrevocably and can cause incredible emotional anguish and inner conflict" ("Chilling" 44).

Hook's first published story, "Pussycat," which defies the constructs of time and text but still has a relatable plot and characters, appeared in *The Science of Sadness* (1994). This anthology opens with an essay on slipstream fiction by editor Chris Kenworthy titled "The Movement of Hands." In it, Kenworthy states: "Slipstream is dependent upon the heart of the writer. It is not a school of writing, or even a movement, so much as an emergent phenomenon in modern fiction [...] It takes the experimentation, the sense of the strange, and applies that feeling to a writer's perceptions of human relations" (12). Hook told me that being published in the anthology felt like a homecoming, and he realized that what he had been writing *was* slipstream.

For a few years, the UK independent press was dominated by slipstream themes. Kenworthy points to the short stories of Nicholas Royle, Allen Ashley, Gary Couzens, Tim Nickels, and M. John Harrison. The influence is visible nowadays in the fiction of Douglas Thompson and Nina Allan, whose fringe SF novels foreground the exploration of inner space and how coincidence creates models for society to inhabit.

Slipstream fiction is not a genre or a subgenre, per se, and like Kenworthy says, it's not a movement. Slipstream authors often write about the everyday complexity of life, unrestrained by convention. They write about relationships and concepts of (un)reality in fantastical, illogical, surreal, ambitious, unsettling, even gruesome ways. In *The Wind-Up Bird Chronicle* (1994), for instance, Haruki Murakami depicts an unreal, mesmeric underworld beneath Tokyo's seemingly normal, docile exterior, estranging readers and challenging our expectations. In *Cloud Atlas* (2004), David Mitchell channels Murakami; he blends SF, metanarration, and historical and contemporary fiction to explore the actions of individuals and their butterfly effects on the past, present, and future across centuries. Both novels are slipstream paradigms that evoke primal emotions while taking narrative risks. According to American novelist Maile Meloy, "Mitchell's book seemed like everything I couldn't do. It's a nested box of stories, each one a virtuosic performance in an entirely different style from the last."

There's also Kurt Vonnegut Jr.'s inimitable dystopian gaze at the world(s) in his ironic masterpiece *Slaughterhouse-Five* (1969) as well as China Miéville's *Perdido Street Station* (2000) and *The City & the City* (2009). All three of these elusive slipstream novels bend genres into hyperreal pretzels. Iain Banks' *The Bridge* (1986), too, is an evocative slipstream work, dark and experimental in its odyssey through the visions of a comatose amnesiac. Banks takes readers on a journey of self-discovery. He also leads us from no-place to no-place. *The Bridge* is mysterious and abstract, playful and impossible, a blur of boundaries and perspectives—all to the book's credit.

Slipstream fiction is a cousin to bizarro fiction, a contemporary literary genre of extreme satire, absurdity, and transgression. Both genres see authors take risks, and while bizarro can be traced back to the work of fledgling authors published by independent presses—see Eraserhead Press's *The Bizarro Starter Kit* (2006)—these days, it's difficult for neophytes to break in. Publishers and editors are less willing to take a gamble, especially on authors who don't define their product within strict genre boundaries. Similar apprehensions befall slipstream fiction, although the parameters are much broader, and unlike bizarro, slipstream can materialize in different genres and in multiple ways.

To me, there's no method to slipstream fiction. What I see is ambitiousness and curiosity in writing, open-mindedness and immersion in reading. Above all, I see an invitation to uncoded artistic expression.

Remember "Borges and I":

It would be an exaggeration to say that ours is a hostile relationship; I live, let myself go on living, so that Borges may contrive his literature, and this literature justifies me. It is no effort for me to confess that he has achieved some valid pages, but those pages cannot save me, perhaps because what is good belongs to no one, not even to him, but rather to the language and to tradition. Besides, I am destined to perish, definitively, and only some instant of myself can survive in him. (211)

References

Bacon, Eugen and Andrew Hook. "Messier 94." *Danged Black Thing.* Transit Lounge Publishing, 2021.

Borges, Jorge Luis. "Borges and I." *Labyrinths: Selected Stories and Other Writing.* Penguin Books, 1964.

Clute, John. "Slipstream SF." *The Encyclopedia of Science*

Fiction. August 10, 2012. Online. October 23, 2021.

Hook, Andrew. "Chilling Out with Andrew Hook." *Aurealis* 138 (March 2021): 42-48.

Kenworthy, Chris. "The Movement of Hands." *The Science of Sadness*. Barrington Books, 1994.

Meloy, Maile. "*Cloud Atlas* a Series of Virtuosic, Soaring Stories." *NPR.com*. November 6, 2007. Online. Accessed June 16, 2021.

INHABITATION
Genni and I

The morning sun, shy and warming—and unwarming—picks up shade from the brown leaves of a tree on a forlorn street shrouded in a town's despair. A hesitant breeze turns her eyes to the entwinement of branch and metal. Does the tree need the streetlight more, or is it the pillar that needs the tree's touch, its unfurling of whispers, little by little, asking if there's ever a yearning to leave?

I'm back in my apartment after an hour's walk around the Tan Track in Melbourne where I navigated joggers and walkers, masks on faces, keeping the right social distance in the permitted exercise quota for Stage 4 pandemic restrictions.

In this solitude of self, in this yearning for the other, I affirm that no woman is an island.

And I call Genni.

Eugen: What language do you dream in?

Genni: I dream in English, but it's not my first language. I think in English; it's never a translation. Swearing is another matter! When I'm cross, I curse in Swahili: *Ng'ombe mjinga! Mbuzi nyang'au!*

E: Do you wonder about betwixt?

G: *Loh!* I'm surprised you ask me this question. You're a scholar and an artist who was once a scientist. You write across forms: short stories, poetry, novels, nonfiction. You write across genres. You're an African, now an Australian, who once lived in the UK and writes for readers around the world—mostly in the US and the UK. With your dualities and multiplicities, between worlds across the self and other, you ask about betwixt?

E: I think I'm wondering about duality. Does duality fracture the self?

G: Let me tell you a story. I was born in a town at the foot of Mount Kilimanjaro. I inherited something from my African mother—her *derrière*. Please don't laugh; I'm going somewhere with this … This bum of mine. Growing up, I really loathed it. But one day it dawned on me. I realized it wasn't going to pack its bags and get a post code of its own. I was stuck with it, and it was mine. It's funny how you change when you grow older. Now I choose clothes that bring it out—it's an asset. I accepted this appendage that was part of me.

As with this bum, we don't get to choose our cultural multiplicities. Every individual develops a unique relationship with the world, a relationship whose distinctive situation is not closed with respect to other cultures that inscribe us.

Like you, as an African Australian migrant, I am a person who experiences an amplified form of hybridity. My sense of "otherness'" is a result of constant immersion in mixed cultures. You wrote about this, Eugen.

The language I have inherited and matured underpins the meaning I assign to any text. My lived experience is rooted in different worlds. This *difference* pervades my everyday life and is integral to my identity and voice(s). It's the sum of who I am.

E: But is duality conflicting?

G: It can be, yes. As an African Australian, I grappled with matters of identity in those early years—I was trying to be African, trying to be Australian. No one came up to me and said, "Can't you be both?" I had to figure this out for myself.

And I guess this is how I fell into speculative fiction, which is a fiction of the strange. In exploring my curiosity about myself and the world, in bending genres and subgenres, I found myself creating worlds where I didn't have to ask the questions: *What color are my characters? What languages do they speak?*

In speculative fiction, I could write a different kind of story constrained only by imagination. I found pleasure in the resistance to the parameters of traditional genre, which meant destabilization, crossing boundaries, allying myself with Deleuze and Guattari's schizoanalytic lines of flight in works like *Anti-Oedipus* (1972) and *A Thousand Plateaus* (1980).

E: Is this different kind of story what draws you to speculative fiction?

G: Yes. Over the decades, speculative fiction has granted authors like Octavia E. Butler the foundations to cultivate inclusive worlds and characters. Eugen, you wrote about this in your book *Writing Speculative Fiction* (2019).

Speculative fiction is a safe place to explore my dualities, my multiplicities. I can use art with subversive activism to interrogate What If? stories that look at social justice and injustice, at equality and equity, spotlighting inner and outer biases. I can write thought experiments that focus on black protagonists, paying attention to black stories in all their possibilities.

I'm particularly delighted to see the rise of black voices in Afrofuturism, a term generally applied to speculative fiction that reimagines black futures and illuminates a new vision of Africa and the diaspora. Butler is sometimes called the mother of Afrofuturism. I share her blackness and identify with her experience. As a young woman, she saw herself as an *other* in the books she read. Butler finally decided to "write herself in" because those stories did not feature marginalized people like her. She wrote speculative fiction about change, sexism, power, and politics, with black heroines in novels like *Fledgling* (2005), which features a young vampire girl, and *Parable of the Sower* (1993), a dystopia set in futuristic Southern California where an African American woman, Lauren Oya Olamina, must negotiate a collapsing society affected (and infected) by inequality and climate change.

Speculative fiction offers a place for me to feel safe even when I examine complex and unsettling themes. My exploratory narratives draw balance and energy from theorists like Roland Barthes, who found pleasure in the text, and for whom the text is a multi-dimensional space where "things are made and unmade," where "language is infinite" and literature is a "deepening and extension of language" (105, 122). I'm interested in the interaction between the work and its characters, the self and the world. My writing is a bridge between internal and external realms.

E: What would you say to purists who think speculative fiction is an adulteration of traditional genre fiction like science fiction, fantasy, and horror?

G: *Pfft.* I'd say, "Get over it." The world is not black and white. Genre labelling is increasingly a device of commercialization. Few readers go to bookstores looking for the latest science fiction, or the latest fantasy, or the latest horror. They want the latest King, Atwood, Jemisin, etc. King in particular is clever—he knowingly writes across genres and blends them together. *The Shining* (1977) is a good example. There are science fiction themes (time and space travel), and fantasy (magical realism) emerges in the titular concept. And, of course, there's horror.

A good writer will stay curious, exploratory, immersed in a creative space that is always redefining itself. A good reader will find affection in deviants and liberation in the wonderment of speculative fiction, especially the kind that avoids pedantic effluences.

E: Give me an example of some black speculative fiction you write.

G: For me, black speculative fiction is a longing, a memory. Here's an excerpt from my short story, "When the Water Stops." First published in the May 2021 issue of *The Magazine of Fantasy and Science Fiction*, it appears in my short-story collection *Danged Black Thing* (2021):

As the climate turned, it hurled at them bushfires that razed huts to the ground, dust storms that swept away families, drought—all the cattle and sheep gone, reduced to skin, then skeletons. At first, the villagers took turns on the bleed, sharing dreams and fears, understanding that as a people they were the same.

But a typical grown male has a blood volume of just five liters—a forty percent loss is deadly. The threshold thirty-nine percent has only ninety-two percent water in it; the rest is washed away in glucose, hormones, proteins, fats, vitamins, mineral salts, and carbon dioxide. What good is it? CO_2 may induce dizziness, tiredness, restlessness, convulsions, or coma. So, given all the minuses, how much water would be left from a bleed to go around a village?

They sifted the question in their minds while volunteers, having bled for the clan, sucked on cactus leaves and sap, figs and desert ants for four to eight weeks afterward. But still they were not strong enough to take another turn when it arrived. (74)

The story is about what happens when water is so scarce, people must extract it from blood … but whose blood? It's about inequality and who hurts. Another short story, "A Pod of Mermaids," also in *Danged Black Thing*, is about a Norse goddess who sends unlimited futures to little black boys but must find a way to defeat Loki's meddling.

Perhaps I can also share something from another fiction collection, *The Road to Woop Woop and Other Stories* (2020). This excerpt comes from "The Animal I Am." In it, two Black women reminisce and connect the past, present, and future.

"Millet brew?"

"Thank you, Nisa. Mmmhh—sweet water from the gods. Makes everything else taste like hyena piss."

"I told you about champagne and all that, Freya. You and the high life."

"When in Rome?"

"Stupid saying, and it's Melbourne we're in."

"It's the concept, Nisa. It's how we enter stories."

"Concept or not, how is that daughter of yours? She and the white man she married."

"K and C? They are separated."

"Ayah? It was raining goals at the stadium, the day they married. Though the good team was winning, I knew it wasn't a good sign when K tore out of the house in that ivory gown of hers and started digging holes in the backyard. Do you remember what she said?"

"She said, 'How do you last years with a lunatic in your face?' She cried inside her veil as she clawed. 'He will Peter Pan me to death!' she said. But you and I both knew C was no Peter Pan. But that didn't make him a no-good husband, Nisa."

"Do you remember what you said to your daughter as she cried and dug with her nails?"

"I said, 'Bend your fucking knees when you dig.' It's called tough love. The astrocenter assured compatibility. There they were: Aries and Gemini. A great match, right?"

"Wrong."

"Mmhhh—this millet brew is something else. Why don't you pour some more? Stop squeezing it from that calabash like it will kill you to serve it."

"Freya, tell me where to get fresh millet in Hawthorn, then maybe I'll get more generous." (115)

Like much of my short fiction, my cli-fi novel *Mage of Fools* (2022) is set in an Afrofuturistic, socialist country named Mafinga and has a black female protagonist. It's about the spirit of humanity in the face of atrocity.

E: Why do you write?

G: There's a power in narrative. Remember, Eugen, you wrote an essay about how narrative works to help us explore trauma? The essay is about personal narrative reflexivity, an autoethnographic (re)search in which you draw from your own personal feelings of discontinuity and convey an awareness of being between worlds as an African migrant in Australia. You wrote it when your sister Flora died. You used yourself as data to gain self-knowledge in the wake of grief.

So you know that narratives and narrative strategies are crucial to exploring and facilitating the nature of being human. Dominique Hecq looks at the usefulness of psychoanalysis for the creative writer and writing in general. She often writes to answer incipient questions troubling her mind or to relieve some form of anxiety where cause may lack symbolization. In her words, "I write because I must do so, exhilarating, detestable or painful though this might be."

Like Hecq, my writing is a search, a question, a curiosity. My approach to the compositional space is with urgency, with a sense that writing is an active form of speaking that emerges from a neutral position of unknowing, or a subjective position of knowing. I write to *find*.

E: Where's your writing space?

G: In my head, mostly, where I spend time constructing fragments and skeletons of ideas, then sketch them on scraps of paper, anytime, anywhere.

E: What are your writing habits or idiosyncrasies?

G: I am so focused, it's not funny. You understand this, Eugen; you finished a Ph.D. in two-and-a-half years. That's the kind of focus I'm talking about. A project keeps me awake—I must finish it.

E: Writing ritual?

G: I write to white noise, with something buzzing in the background, like news, sport or music. But it's not crucial to my process.

E: Are you a pantser, a plotter, or somewhere in between?

G: Fundamentally, I'm a panster, although I do outline novels and works of nonfiction. My methodology can be random. Sometimes I revisit my short stories, wonder about rewriting them across forms, genres ... I tend to write on a trigger: a sentiment, an idea, a memory.

E: What would you like to improve about your writing?

G: I'd like to be less impatient to get things out. I'm very prolific, and don't know how to sit on things. Nothing niggles me like a deadline.

E: Do you have a writerly crush?

G: I'm madly, deeply in love with Toni Morrison. Ray Bradbury, too. Also, I recently discovered Andrew Hook, a European slipstream-fiction writer. I love his short fiction, especially the collections *Frequencies of Existence* (2020), *The Forest of Dead Children* (2019), *Human Maps* (2016), *Nitrospective* (2011), and *Beyond Each Blue Horizon* (2005).

E: What are you reading right now?

G: Did I tell you about Andrew Hook?

E: You do know me, intimately …

G: But, of course.

E: One last question … Who do you say you are, really?

G: I am a mother, an artist, a writer, a reader. I am a sum of parts. I am many, betwixt, a fusion of cultures. I am the self and the other, a story of inhabitation, a multiple embodiment.

And, as you know, I am you, painted in shadows …

References

Bacon, Eugen. "The Animal I Am." *The Road to Woop Woop and Other Stories*. Meerkat Press, 2020.

———. "When the Water Stops." *Danged Black Thing*. Transit Lounge Publishing, 2021.

Barthes, Roland. *The Grain of the Voice: Interviews (1962-1980)*. Hill & Wang, 1985.

Hecq, Dominique. "Writing the Unconscious: Psychoanalysis for the Creative Writer." *TEXT* 12.2 (October 2008): Online. Accessed September 20, 2020.

Rosaldo, Renato. *Culture & Truth: The Remaking of Social Analysis*. Beacon Press, 1993.

BLACK IS NOT BLAK

Overnight my mobile phone goes from ivory white to blood red, trembling and humming cautions, reprimands, censures, admonitions, allegories of broken trust in notification after notification from yet another faceless avatar.

I turn the device to silent, but it's a transient lineament, a limitation that doesn't patch a world breaking in a winter already come, ready or not, in the maw of Melbourne's toughest restrictions yet. I am alone in a metropolis deep in a state of disaster. Lockdown has taken a new turn with nightly curfews and five-kilometer travel restrictions, and only for four reasons: work, care, exercise, and shopping.

My son is staying with his father in an outer suburb. Part of me misses him, but I'm thankful he's away at a time when my world is beneath a tower of tombstones. Stone on stone. Cold.

This is a migrant's story.

Mask-wearing, exercising, even the simplest tasks are furthest from my mind. I study the ceiling from my bed, joining cracks and shadows. My head chimes with voices, drills, and dryers. The door is ajar. But my isolation is a coffin built for one, closed all over. I clutch my throat and understand how one might contemplate the gape of a tomb.

Does rigor mortis bring a quieting of pain? My innards are dissolving, bugs with masks crawling to fill that space. Spills and slips—I am years from myself—a lost girl searching for a hymn or a whale song in the wind.

I long to seize the day, but boundaries confine my reach. This sense of disparity ... my belief is gone. Relative to the black fiction at the core of all this agita, am I a victim of context or the culprit of my own character?

I consider phoning my brother, talking him through my current tribulations, but I don't know if he'll understand. The cultural and physical distance between Melbourne and Dar-es-Salaam is too big. My sister has just shaken COVID. She didn't need to ask; I sent her money so she could eat healthy foods. I won't burden her with my story. My other brother is planning a wedding for his son. My other sister is making do after her husband's retirement. Now is not the time to turn to family with a cry.

Or am I so reclusive with my writing career and my juggling act as a single mum that I've closed off my support network?

The phone keeps pinging. Warnings, reprimands on Twitter from people I don't know. I start muting conversations, but the phone won't stop. Each avalanche of messages spikes my sense of aloneness, of trepidation. These are Blak people, I tell myself. We are kindred. Australia is a country we both call home. Any harm was unintentional. Why are they so unkind and antagonistic to me? But it's not just me. The book's artist is also getting malevolent tweets.

During a lap around Melbourne's Tan Track, I realize what I must do. I'm not so fragile that I might step off a roof from cyber messaging. I could block the persistent ones, de-activate my Twitter account.

I email the UK publisher and he says, yes, he's aware of these matters. Emails are flooding in with concerns about the book's title (something to do with dreaming) and elements of the cover that look like Indigenous Australian art.

The publisher supports me. Together we work out a strategy and decide to (1) rename the book, (2) retrieve elements from the cover that might be construed as Indigenous, and (3) run a sweep of the text to make sure it holds no suggestion of cultural appropriation.

Ivory's Story told its own story, but it would also tell a story about me.

With my African heritage, and as a migrant in Australia, I understood that there was a lot I needed to learn about Indigenous culture. I remained curious about intertextuality, about deep connections between texts, genres, and forms. I understood that there are multiple points of intersection in blackness, and the book cover was designed by a South African artist intimately familiar with my African culture.

My intention was to write a black speculative-fiction novel; set in Australia, it would be a murder mystery as well as an origin tale, and it would incorporate African themes. Ivory Tembo, the female protagonist, was a mixed-race woman, very much like my own son. On the book cover, her eyes are shut: in the context of the narrative, she inhabits a hypnogogic space, somewhere between sleep and wakefulness. Her face bears traditional markings that are also African, aligned with traditional war paint, dance paint, wooing paint …

People from the African diaspora who read and reviewed the book were struck by its closeness to their own cultures. One Nigerian author appreciated the common themes and knowledge we shared from our ancestral origin. She understood the superstition, the dumping of twins at the edge of the forest (we call it the bad forest: *Ajo-ofia*, she said), the romance of the female sun and the male moon, the use of nuts by witchdoctors …

I looked at the draft statement that the organization for which I served as Board Director had shown me prior to its public release:

> The ___ does not condone any appropriation of Indigenous cultural heritage, including iconography, symbolism, art or traditional stories. We deeply respect Indigenous cultural heritage and understand that this heritage is owned by relevant Traditional Owners throughout Australia.
>
> We are aware that the cover and title of an upcoming book by ___ Board Director … offended members of the community on the basis it appropriated Indigenous culture … deeply regrets this matter, and has learnt from it. She has publicly apologized and offered her resignation from the Board, which has been accepted …
>
> The ___ has, and continues to recommend to all non-Indigenous authors, when writing about or using Indigenous cultural material, to reflect on their work and to meaningfully consult and collaborate with First Nations people who are represented in the narration before proceeding to publication.

My publication did not include representations of First Nations people. The organization's stance had made my position on the Board untenable. We tried to salvage the situation, but the organization wanted more action than I could promise. They wanted me to withhold or withdraw the publication and consult with Indigenous peoples.

The organization was coming from a place of blindness.

What about my culture? Nothing in the book referenced an Aboriginal place, character, or community.

Yes, there were fictitious black people in the novel, like Ginny, a medicine woman who Ivory called "my mother," which is the African way. In addition, I deployed Swahili and Bantu traditions that reflected my African Australian "betwixt." *Tembo* is the Swahili name for elephant. *Buntu* is a being in my mother tongue. *Ubuntu* means community spirit in South Africa. *Bahati* means luck in Swahili. Kurwa and Dotto are what we call twins in my culture, shortened in the story to Ku and Doh.

I guess a part of me was disillusioned with the organization because all this was happening at a time when the Board was talking about increasing diversity. It felt like the executive committee had chosen to save face with a hanging tree: one Black for the greater Blak.

But Black is not Blak.

Black in Australia is different from black in the diaspora and the United States.

The Australian Museum estimates at least 270 frontier massacres—state-sanctioned efforts to eradicate First Nations people. Colonial genocide actions saw 1.5 million First Nations people plummet to less than 100,000 by the early 1900s (Sentence).

Australia has apologized in multiple ways for the horrific treatment of Indigenous people by white people. Survival Day (also called Invasion or Australia Day) on January 26 is a day of mourning for Aboriginal and Torres Strait Islander peoples. Apology Day on February 13 is a national act of contrition for past laws, policies, and practices that harmed Indigenous Australians. National Sorry Day on May 26 extends this apology in an annual remembrance of those adverse policies that forcibly removed children from their families. Celebrated between May 27 and June 3, National Reconciliation Week commemorates a successful 1967 referendum that recognizes Aboriginal and Torres Strait Islander peoples as integral to Australia. NAIDOC week, in the beginning of July, celebrates Indigenous history, culture, and achievements.

For all of these apologies, Indigenous disadvantage remains palpable in Australia. *The Guardian* published a report on new data in 2020 suggesting that there have been over 430 Aboriginal deaths in police custody since the 1990s alone. A National Sorry Day didn't stop them.

I told *Ivory's Story* from the complacent perspective of cultural multiplicity. I didn't foresee Australia's warranted sensitivity to matters pertaining to Indigenous peoples. I should have foreseen it, but it escaped me.

My black as a migrant was not a black that Australia understood.

A History

I was born in what was once German East Africa in the late 1800s. This colony in the African Great Lakes region included Burundi, Rwanda, the Kionga Triangle, and most of what is now the United Republic of Tanzania. Germany invaded Africa to establish itself among other European powers, mainly France and Britain. Germans exerted direct rule, unlike their British counterparts, who exerted indirect rule—political governance that acknowledged Europeans and Africans as inherently different and ascertained that Africans were best ruled through their own pre-existing power structures of chieftaincy, kingdoms, or native authorities (i.e., "protectorates").

Unlike the "truce" of protectorates that nudged the building of schools, railroads, and hospitals, the German direct rule exploited Africa. The conquest arrived with bloodshed, witnessed in the Maji Maji Rebellion, where Africans revolted against German colonialists who were forcing the growth of cotton for export. Africans stood no chance with their limited weaponry and belief of magic water from the witchdoctor Kinjeketile, who promised that sacred *maji* ("water" in Swahili) would protect black people from white men's bullets. It didn't work. The Maji Maji Uprising or Rebellion (1905-1907) saw approximately 75,000 Africans die from fighting, disease, and hunger, the latter from the destruction of crops and farmland by Germans (Iliffe 495).

The mainland country became a British mandate in 1916 after Germany was stripped of its colonies at the end of World War I. The new territory was named Tanganyika. It gained independence in 1961 and united with the island of Zanzibar, a former British colony, in 1964 to form what is now Tanzania (Rosenne 224).

My mother gave birth to me in a town at the foot of Mount Kilimanjaro. My father's career took my family to Kenya when I was two years old. I visited my grandparents' village by traveling across Lake Victoria by ferry to an island, then walking and riding from the port along dusty roads to my grandmother's hut. A woman of her time, she couldn't read or write, and even when cultural limitation ebbed, she never ate or drank anything that was deemed food for a man: milk, meat, eggs, and fish.

As a young girl, my mother ran barefoot to and from school, determined to earn her place in the world. She eventually found that place and became a schoolteacher. Growing up, our house was always surrounded by children.

You never could tell by looking which child belonged to my mother. We all called her Mama.

Years later, my own studious ambition got the best of me. I earned a scholarship to the University of Greenwich in the United Kingdom and completed a M.Sc. degree with distinction in Distributed Computer Systems. I lived and worked in London for a few years in an IT department at New Scotland Yard, then migrated to Melbourne with my then Aussie husband and my young child.

My romance with the white man's world was full of stoppage. Like Mama, I fought hard for my place in that world, and it took the M.Sc. degree, a new M.A. degree, and a Ph.D. to finally land a senior role in the office. I knew I could go harder and go longer than my white-skinned, blue-eyed colleagues. Nonetheless, they rose higher than me in the workplace.

As a black person, I felt wounded every time I didn't get a job or promotion. It hurt when the judicial system nearly got it wrong with my mixed-race child. I fought for his custody because my color was "wrong" and his father's color was "right." It pierced me to the core when a stranger on the street called me "Zimbabwe." It sliced me to the bone when someone on the tram addressed me as Barack Obama's sister. It undid me from head to toe when my child came home from school one day and asked me with big eyes and a small voice: "What color is best, Mama? What color is *the best color*?"

It took time to embrace my duality as African Australian. Finally, I gave myself permission to write about my culture in black fiction that had characters who looked like me. Octavia Butler and Toni Morrison had done it. Now it was my turn.

When *Ivory's Story* started all that trouble, it was a blow, a knife. I felt shame, a compounding of unbelonging. Trust was broken. I was broken.

I didn't expect consolation or support from anybody.

The first R U OK? email arrived from someone who wasn't an actual friend. We were connected on social media. I'd tried to be strong in my isolation, holding it together, doing the right thing despite feeling depressed and inadequate. But this rogue email shifted my spirits. For the first time in a long time, I felt warmer inside.

I received more emails from strangers. Soon I had pen pals with whom I wrote back and forth. They gave me courage, strength, and optimism.

I published an apology and pinned it on my reactivated Twitter account. Just like that, the notifications stopped. The world forgot. But I remember it like it was yesterday.

Ivory's Story was published in 2020. It was well-received and shortlisted in the British Science Fiction Association Awards. I'm curious about the perspectives of readers who know enough about African cultures and traditions to see them in the novella and recognize the dichotomies. Reviews indicate that many people get it. The black protagonist has a big story. Award-winning South African writer Nick Wood wrote this commendation for the novella: "Bacon expertly weaves a speculative world with harsh and mundane realities to form a lush and magical tale about the importance of love and the courage needed to face the demons of this world and the next. Highly recommended." *Publishers Weekly* had this to say:

> Bacon masterfully blends together myth, heritage, and self-discovery in this impressive, genre-defying work

of speculative fiction. African Australian detective Ivory Tembo searches for the culprit of a horrifying series of murders in Sydney […] In order to prevent more slaughter and protect her lover's life, Ivory must break a curse, and discovers along the way that some legends are all-too-real. Writing with sharp, insightful prose, Bacon delivers a taut thriller that dives deep into its distinctive protagonist's internal life and family history. Seasoned speculative fiction readers will be wowed by Bacon's careful, layered worldbuilding, well-developed characters, and otherworldly atmosphere. This deserves a wide audience.

Ironically, it was mostly people who'd never read the book that misunderstood it.

I have reflected upon this experience for a long time, and one thing is very clear: it's essential for there to be frank and ongoing discussions about colonization, othering, and appropriation. Sometimes these conversations are necessarily challenging and uncomfortable.

Something else has become clear.

There is an awkwardness between African migrants and First Nations people, Australia's dominant black groups. We don't know how to navigate each other, and perhaps there's built-in mistrust. We shouldn't be suspicious of our differences. Inside these differences are notable similarities.

We need to recognize how we have been conditioned to be at odds and move past it.

One has a sense of belonging: Indigenous Australians have been on the land since the beginning.

One has a fear of unbelonging: migrants are naturalized—but we aren't drifters who float through the social and cultural matrix, who come in cold, with no history.

Similarities and Differences

The first major genomic study of Aboriginal Australians was published in 2016. Conducted by an international team of academics in collaboration with leaders from Aboriginal Australian communities, the study "points to one shared 'Out of Africa' migration" for modern humans and suggests that, like all non-Africans, Aboriginal Australians can trace their ancestry back to a massive exodus from Africa 72,000 years ago ("Unprecedented").

Moreover, the study determines that the descendants of Indigenous Peoples were the first to leave Africa and migrate to Asia and Australia. Aboriginal Australians are closer in genetic inheritance to the ancient South Asians, and they have more similarities with Papuans than Africans do. Hence the visible difference in our skin tone and hair texture. Physically, we are different.

But there are cultural and historical similarities as well as multiple points of intersection. We are Bla(c)k Australians. We have both seen the worst of white people. They have colonized and enslaved us, snatched our rights and our babies. They have massacred hundreds of thousands of our people. They have made us feel less equal for the dark color of our skin.

We have cultural intersections. Kinship and community relations inform our responsibilities to the family unit, to our clan, to our society, to the world.

We have similarities in some cultural artifacts. Traditional markings on African art closely resemble Indigenous art.

We understand the importance of language, of story, the passing of knowledge and folklore from generation to generation through oral tradition, teaching our culture, values, beliefs, and history.

We treasure clans, our sense of ancestry. We respect our elders. We assign importance to naming. We see meaning in land. We have an affinity with nature (trees, animals, water). We have cleansing and exorcising rituals. We have an intrinsic belief in spirituality, cultural concepts of life and the afterlife.

But Africa is not a country. Migrants in Australia may comprise any of the primary groups of Bantus, Nilotes, or Cushites. Migrants may come from any of the 54 countries in Africa. They may speak any of the 2,000 languages: Swahili, Amharic, Yoruba, Oromo, Hausa, Igbo, Zulu, Shona, even Arabic, French, Portuguese ... They may be any of the 1.378 billion peoples from the continent, accustomed to cassava, millet, sorghum, maize, yams, papaya, coconuts ... and now learning the taste of an Aussie barbie.

There's also diversity within Aboriginal and Torres Strait Islander Peoples—hundreds of languages and dialects between them; unique contrasts in cultures between groups; expanded networks of relationships through kinship, intermarriage, or geographical location ...

But we are Bla(c)k and we are Australian.

We understand family. We celebrate birth, death, rites of passage. There are hurdles to overcome, like the specter of ethnocentrism. There is an answer somewhere, a bridge that crosses an invisible gorge separating two Bla(c)k peoples ...

Melbourne's lockdown is over.

I survived.

I hope this precarious relationship will survive, too ...

References

Iliffe, John. "The Organization of the Maji Maji Rebellion." *Journal of African History* 8.3 (1967): 495-512.

Review of *Ivory's Story*. *Publishers Weekly*. November 6, 2020. Online. Accessed November 5, 2021.

Rosenne, Shabtai. *Documents of the International Court of Justice*. Sijthoff, 1974.

Sentence, Nathan. "Genocide in Australia." *Australian Museum*. May 26, 2020. Online. Accessed November 9, 2021.

"Unprecedented Study of Aboriginal Australians Points to One Shared Out of Africa Migration for Modern Humans." *University of Cambridge: Research News*. September 21, 2016. Online. Accessed November 7, 2021.

THE BENEFIT OF OUR HUMANITY

An adult skeleton has 206 bones and 32 teeth, but did you know that babies are born with 300 mixtures of bone and cartilage? The cartilage hardens into bone during a process called ossification.

Blood is essential to human life. It circulates throughout our bodies in plasma, red blood cells, white blood cells, and platelets, distributing oxygen, vitamins, glucose, and amino acids that combine to make muscle-building proteins. Blood transports metabolic waste, including unwanted salts, phosphates, sulphates, and urea from our cells. A red blood cell has a lifecycle of 120 days in the body. Platelets control our bleeding, so we don't bleed out, and white blood cells help protect us against disease.

In genetics, there are dominant and recessive alleles. Each human cell carries two copies of each chromosome, and each version of the gene is called an allele. A dominant allele (it overwhelms a recessive one) is responsible for brown eye color, broad nose, freckles, and curly hair. Recessive alleles (you need two of them) are responsible for hazel eye color, narrow nose, white skin, and straight hair. A child doesn't have the privilege of choosing what gene it gets. Whatever it gets comes from the fusion of a sperm and an egg to form a diploid cell called a zygote. And it's mildly complicated for mixed-race people like my son.

When you fall in love, your body releases a rush of dopamine, producing pleasurable, often euphoric feelings. Adrenaline increases blood flow from your heart to trigger the pleasure center of your brain. Norepinephrine also speeds up your heart and heightens the thrill. Your brain and body change, and you want to cuddle, you want to hug, you want to kiss. The object of your affection instills a sense of calm and security. Your blood pressure decreases; you feel less anxiety. You get butterflies in your stomach.

When you die, your brain cells shut down—they have no blood flow. In the throes of dying, you lose hunger and thirst, then speech, then vision. The last senses to go are hearing and touch. You would hear the last words of your killer if they called you a nigger as you died. This might have been the last words Ahmaud Arbery heard after being chased, hunted, and executed by Travis McMichael as Arbery lay breathless on the crimson-stained ground, nauseated, his kidney, liver, heart, lungs, and brain slowly shutting down.

Black and white babies are both born with 300 mixtures of bone and cartilage. White babies don't get any more bones or cartilage than black ones: blood flows in both just the same. They each inherit two alleles and have no say in what eye color they get. Black and white people fall in love the same. When they die, their bodies shut off the same before they start going through autolysis or self-digestion, as their oxygen-deprived cells increase in acidity and their enzymes begin to digest cell membranes and leak out. Their skin discolors, their body temperature drops, and rigor mortis sets in, starting in the eyelids, jaws, and neck muscles. As the corpse begins to release 30 or so different chemicals, the gases and compounds produced during the decomposition process exude the rotten smell of death.

Black and white people smell the same when they die. Dead white people don't smell like honeysuckle or stargazer lilies. Not all live white people smell that good either. I've met dirty white people who stink like unwashed socks. And there are goalless white people who wouldn't know motivation if it plummeted from the sky and landed on their heads. Narcissistic white people, too—she was a kiwi, a total bitch. Cost me my job. This doesn't mean that all white people are dirty, or goalless, or narcissistic. But white people are human, as are black people.

Black lives matter—this is the global chant that calls attention to the humanity of black people in the wake of escalating events in the United States. Emmet Till was lynched like a puppet in Money, Mississippi, in 1955 for looking at a white woman—he was human, and he felt everything. Amadou Diallo was shot and killed like a dog by four New York City plainclothes police officers who unloaded 41 bullets into his body—he was human. Ahmaud Arbery went out for a jog in Brunswick, Georgia, and was hunted like a deer, shot in broad daylight—he was human. Breonna Taylor, killed by police officers in Louisville, Kentucky—

she was an emergency medical technician, only 26 when she died, shot at least eight times like a pheasant for sport in her own apartment under the pretense of a no-knock search warrant for another person. She was human, but her killers have not been charged with a crime. And George Floyd was human when he suffocated in Minneapolis, Minnesota, begging the officer who drove a knee into the back of his neck for air. "I can't breathe," George wheezed … and died.

Of course, racism is not confined to the US and its history of enslaving black people. Australia has a shameful legacy (less scrutinized compared to racism in the US) in its treatment of Aboriginal people. A National Sorry Day won't bring back the stolen generation. This is the horrific capacity of the human condition. Snatch children from their mothers' breasts in the name of racial supremacy and assimilation. Forcibly remove them from their black families. Surround them with whiteness to protect them from becoming more "native."

I am a mother of a colored child. I see him as caramel; others may only see black. I don't want to lose this boy to racism. I don't want him hurt by a judicial system created to "protect" him, by a police officer with an eager baton, keen rubber bullets, tasers, or gas masks. We need to hold people in authority accountable. We need to hold our leaders accountable. Most of all, we need to hold ourselves accountable.

What, when, and where is racism today? Is it a thing of the past or an ever-evolving monster of the future? Ask yourself this question when you're shortlisting candidates for a job. Ask yourself this question when you're assessing applications for a business loan. Ask yourself this question when you're wondering how best to "safely" introduce your partner of color to your family. Ask yourself this question when you're out jogging in your neighborhood and no one is hunting you down with shotguns like an animal, as they did Mr. Arbery.

Ask yourself these questions: How often do people give you a wary eye for the color of your skin? How often do people ask you where you are from even though you're right where you belong? Do you feel compelled to write under a pseudonym, withhold your profile photo, or use an icon, lest your native-sounding name and colored face are not relatable to a particular readership? Does the supermarket guard reliably ask you to open your bag because he thinks you might have stolen something? Does airport security frequently pull you aside for a chemical test? That sweet old lady clutching her bag and walking faster, hastily taking a detour when you stroll behind her—is it because you "look" suspect?

Racism is when your son comes home from school with big eyes, looks at himself in the mirror, and asks you in a small voice "what color is best" because some bully said something about his appearance. Racism is when, years later, some white girl won't date him because he's black but others will because he's "exotic." Racism is when strangers call you "Zimbabwe" (despite your real birthplace) or Barack Obama's sister (despite having no relationship with or connection to the Obamas). Racism is when you're exceedingly qualified for a job that goes to a white person because they're a "better fit." Racism is any discrimination against somebody who doesn't look like you, speak like you—black, yellow, or white.

This is one way to make it right: acknowledge the harm. If you're thinking you don't want to go there—*please go there.* Emerge from the margins, take a stand. Doing nothing is being complicit. *Do better* for black people. Do better for ethnic minorities. We are your friends, your partners, your colleagues. It's time to listen, to hear pleas that say, "We are done dying. We are done surviving. We want to live."

Black lives matter—not because others don't, but *because others won't if black lives don't.*

"Do not think there are no crocodiles just because the water's calm." Black people have many proverbs like this one, passed down from elders we respect. We raise our children to have values, and we ask our ancestors to guide them. Another proverb goes: "He that beats the drum for the mad man to dance is no better than the mad man himself." We need great leaders of the modern world, people like Nelson Mandela, Martin Luther King Jr., and Abraham Lincoln. Amid the racial unsettlement impacting the US and the rest of us, our world is also subject to the buffoonery of America's political experiment, which may be the work of the dumbest mad scientist to ever exist in fiction or reality.

We are done with misguided leadership. If you're a leader with a brain the size of a rat, a mouth the size of Uranus, now is the time to shut up and not tweet.

And you voters, you are beholden to the world—it's your right, and ours, that you choose leaders of character, people with ethics.

Science says that black and white people are the same. Please, oh please, let's stay on top of it. Give us the benefit of our humanity.

This article is a tribute to Black Lives Matter.

MAKING *CLAIMING T-MO*
A Black Speculative Fiction

Bronwyn Lovell's review of *Claiming-T-Mo* (2019) in *TEXT* assigns scholarly value to my black speculative-fiction novel. She grounds the review in literary theory, linking the novel with feminist theory in particular. "*Claiming T-Mo* acts as a critique of patriarchy and an extended meditation on masculinities," Lovell writes. "It explores the ways women are hurt and haunted by the men they love—as partners, fathers, and sons. It is also testament to the resilience and potentially transformative power of women's love in the face of patriarchal terror" (3).

This kind of academic scrutiny brings me back to the book's genesis. It was a product of my Ph.D. in creative writing. As I worked towards the degree, I became increasingly preoccupied with not only crossing genres, but with manifesting a literary style. I wanted to write something about difference, about otherness, and about the plight of women. At the same time, I wanted to scrutinize embodiment, the nature of being, the "self," and how to exist simultaneously in/between worlds.

This is the story of how I conceived and composed *Claiming T-Mo*.

What I Sought to Produce

Early in the novel, I introduced the illusive, elusive nature of my titular character and their world(s):

> T-Mo happened exactly one week after the puzzle-piece woman with fifty-cent eyes.
>
> One night, black as misery, Salem Drew stood, arms wrapped about herself, at the bus depot three streets from the IGA where she worked late shifts. A bunch of commuters had just clambered onto a number 146 for Carnegie, and Salem found herself alone at the depot.
>
> She waited for a night express bus to take her back to a cheerless home that housed equally cheerless parents. An easy wind around her was just as dreary, foggy as lunacy. There, just then, the shadow of a woman's face jumped into her vision.
>
> Salem blinked. Was the woman real or a figment of thought? Singular parts of her were easy to file, were possibly real: maroon hair, rugged skin the color of coffee beans. And the scar … But all put together, cohesion was lost. (3)

I approached the project with an understanding that external influences imprint my artistic formations: family, self-experience, education, culture, society … The language I speak (and write) influences and exposes my preconditioning.

I sought to break the boundaries of conventional fiction with speculative fiction, which allows "extraordinary" storytelling in figurative as well as literal senses of the word. The possibilities in speculative fiction seemed limitless to me. There were no boundaries; I felt like I could do anything, go anywhere, unhindered by the "rules" of "good writing."

My Ph.D. dissertation took the form of a literary speculative novel accompanied by an exegesis in practice-led research. Serving as a template for my guidebook *Writing Speculative Fiction* (2019), the exegesis explained the birth of the creative artifact and positioned itself between this artifact and the audience to clarify my methodology. Together, the exegesis and the novel shaped my pursuit of a broader experiential and contextualized approach to writing.

I undertook the study with two research questions linked to "writing different."

1. Can a writer of short fiction productively apply a model of stories-within-a-story to build a novel, and if so, what techniques or experiences are transferable from one form to the other?
2. Does literary writing contribute to the quality of science fiction, fantasy, or speculative fiction?

Using the model of stories-within-a-story for *Claiming T-Mo,* I aspired to create purposeful adaptations and embedded vignettes amounting to a cohesive novel that was almost like a story-cycle; the arrangement of the stories, thematic ties, and collective protagonists held the texts together. The overarching narrative flowed smoothly from one point to another, with each embedded part bearing a concealed self-sufficiency interlinked and layered into the composite whole.

I paid attention to speculative fiction comprised of embedded stories carefully placed within the novel, continuing rather than expanding them. As I moved from one story to the next, I layered the novel with characters, timelines, motifs, and interplay—a sum of parts.

I researched story-cycles; borrowing from the concept of Deleuze and Guattari's rhizome, I produced "circles of convergence" and "lines of flight [and] rupture" (22). I became fascinated with the art of language and enjoyed playing with words. I took lessons from theorists like Roland Barthes, who found pleasure in the text, and for whom the text is a multi-dimensional space where "things are made and unmade," where "language is infinite" and literature is a "deepening and extension of language" (105, 122). And I turned to existentialists like Simone de Beauvoir, who understood the power of literature, particularly the degree to which a novel and its characters help us better understand ourselves and the absurdities of the world at large.

Shaping the Novel

I approached the novel and its characters from the perspective of "being different" and a "breed of others" within the context of a traditional quest motif. In *The Writer's Journey* (1998), Christopher Vogler explores the relationship between mythology and storytelling, taking a cue from Joseph Campbell's *The Hero with a Thousand Faces* (1949), a classic study of comparative mythology. Campbell investigates the hero's call to adventure, the road of trials, the vision quest, and ultimately the hero's triumphant return home. For Campbell, myths are the "masks of God" through which people seek to "relate themselves to the wonders of existence" (xx). Campbell took his own cue from Carl Jung's theories of archetypes, the personal and collective unconscious, and the human psyche.

In addition to specialized archetypes like the wolf, the hunter, the wicked stepmother, the fairy godmother, the witch, the prince/ss, and the greedy innkeeper in fairy tales, Vogler identifies recurrent mythic figures, namely the hero (protagonist), but also variants like the antihero (antagonist or villain), the tragic hero (e.g., Macbeth), the catalyst hero (who incites transformation in the other rather than the self), the mentor (wise old man), the threshold guardian (hero's obstacle), the herald (who calls the hero to adventure), and the shapeshifter (a scheming, unstable character).

In light of its composite protagonists, *Claiming T-Mo* does not strictly follow the typical, single-hero, archetypal quest familiar to publishers. Neither Vogler's stages of the hero's journey nor the elaborate plot points for an outline fitted the crafting of my artifact, which is built on a model of stories-within-a-story. Specifically, *Claiming T-Mo* interlinks stories across genres and combines literary writing (e.g., poetic language), soft SF (e.g., time travel and intergalactic odyssey), and fantasy (e.g., magical realism). Moreover, time is complicated and involves chronology, flashbacks, overlaps, even parallelism; and the setting is in Grovea (an alien planet), East Point, Yellow Trek, and Middle Creek (Earth). In short, there are multiple places, time periods, and "interchangeable parts" that together favor narrative schizophrenia over linearity. I wanted *Claiming T-Mo* to be different. I did *not* want it to conform to the rules of any genre or form.

Introducing Characters Along Themes of "Difference" and a Traditional Quest Motif

Major characters in *Claiming T-Mo* include:

> **Silhouette:** Silhouette's story begins in a matriarchal society where a child belongs to its mother, is named by its mother. When husband Novic takes it upon himself to name the child, he initiates chaos that splits the boy in two: T-Mo and Odysseus. This riff on Robert Louis Stevenson's *Dr. Jekyll and Mr. Hyde*

(1886) stages a doubled man whose persona swings from distinguished to repulsive.

Salem Drew: There is a disquieting quality about a man (T-Mo) who steps through locked doors and unbroken walls, who cruises to botanical majesties that look nothing like Earth, whose eyes are full of space when they don't hold something wild. Salem knows this man, and she keeps him at bay. But when space vanishes from T-Mo's eyes and poems appear in their depths, the guardrails of her apprehension fall away.

Myra Lexus: Myra is a hybrid. She struggles to assert her identity in a conformist world. When Vida Stuart comes into her life, more than a gruesome secret binds them.

Tempest Lexus-Stuart: Tempest is a precocious girl. A child who holds an orb of lightning in her fist and a beast in her belly, she tosses her mother Myra into more than bafflement.

Amber: Amber is an off-worlder in familial exile from the land of Xhaust. Now she is orphaned, by bloodline and by soulhood, enriched with a new type of kindred connected to immortality or some aberrant ability.

T-Mo/Odysseus: The titular good/evil multi-person.

Novic: An immortal Sayneth priest.

In building these characters, I was influenced by other authors' applications of the experimental and the adventurous from which my writing borrows. This type of fiction made me feel safe even when I interrogated complex and unsettling themes.

I found early snippets of character sketches in my drafts like this one: "Tempest—Titian red locks. Tiger eyes as fiery as the flaming ruby in her hair. The child's beautiful, loud eyes switched from one face to the other, big yellow eyes that held more curiosity than baby softness, their expression more questioning than accepting, as Myra spoke fondly and delicately brushed back with a finger unruly hair the color of ruby."

Each of my characters, including Tempest, plays a role in interrogating the challenges and possibilities of being different. Most characters, like Myra, find themselves between worlds in dichotomous situations where they could try to "belong" or "be." As a child of multiple cultures myself—a sum of many—it was a theme that was important for me to explore.

As I continued to formulate characters, I turned again to Vogler's mythic structure, which presents storytelling paradigms and a study of character archetypes and quests, such as the hero/ine's journey in 12 stages:

1. Ordinary world
2. Call to adventure (inciting incident)
3. Refusal of the call
4. Meeting with the mentor
5. Crossing the first threshold
6. Tests, allies, enemies
7. Approach to the inmost cave
8. Ordeal (mid-point, death and rebirth)
9. Reward (seizing the sword)
10. The road back
11. Resurrection (climax)
12. Return with the elixir (denouement)

Like Campbell, Vogler siphons Jung, applying the psycho-analyst's template of archetypes to his storytelling model. Vogler identifies a story's effectiveness by the physical way it affects his body: "An effective story grabs your gut, tightens your throat, makes your heart race and your lungs pump, brings tears to your eyes or an explosion of laughter to your lips. If I wasn't getting some kind of physiological reaction from a story, I knew it was only affecting me on an intellectual level and therefore it would probably leave audiences cold" (x).

For my novel to thrive, I sought a transformational arc within which to enfold the stories. This arc arrived in the form of the character Silhouette. Her story is the type of heroine's journey that considers the woman's psychological and spiritual development; Silhouette's transformation in the novel is motivated by an urge to find healing from deep wounding at the hands of two significant males in her life: husband Novic and son Odysseus. She remains the character who haunts other characters across the story, a puzzle-piece woman with maroon hair, rugged skin the color of coffee beans and silver shimmering from "one good eye, petite and round as a fifty-cent coin. The other eye was broken, feasibly some bygone injury. Even though it was as smooth and flawlessly round as the right eye, it held no sight. The coin perfection of its shape was embedded in scar tissue, a disfigurement that needed nothing but a single glance to seal the hideousness of it" (15).

Like the primary characters in the novel, Silhouette stands apart. She is an "other" who wants to belong. She is an omniscient narrator who—from the narrator's point of view—serves as a bridge to the author. She has insight into other characters, observing from within and without, offering inner access to this world and its characters. Her transformational arc closes when she heals at the novel's end.

As the story progresses, Salem follows a separate quest to find meaning. Her life in the ordinary world at East Point with her parents is empty. She meets the otherworldly T-Mo, who becomes her mentor and invites her to cross a threshold into a completely unordinary realm. Then there is an ordeal, the loss of T-Mo, and finally resurrection towards the end.

As I composed the novel, I methodically reflected on what happened in each sequence, what the characters were feeling, where they were going, whether or not the details I used were effective, and how those details might funnel into other parts of the narrative. Like Vogler, I considered the relationship between mythology and storytelling, where "good stories make you feel you've been through a satisfying, complete experience. You've cried or laughed or both" (xxvii–xxviii).

I learned from my characters—from how they engaged with being different, from their searches for meaning and identity. I infused my artifact with elements that bred behavior while haunting my characters' forms and formulae.

The mythological Odysseus figured prominently in my design. In Greek and Roman philosophy, Odysseus is a model of wisdom, a "man of many turns, the most versatile of all Greek heroes both in Homeric epic and in his later incarnations" (Montiglio 1). The end of the novel gestures towards implosion, with T-Mo bleeding into Odysseus, and vice versa. Identity escapes us. We don't know who is who, until, until …

Challenges

At times, the dual roles of being an artist and a scholar made it difficult for me to balance technical and accessible language. As I explored the nature of selfhood within myself and my characters, however, I narrowed down and refined my scope, and I increasingly concentrated voice and tone. Eventually I became comfortable with this hybrid creative/critical impetus.

The short story is the backbone of everything I write. This longer piece posed a significant challenge. I taught myself to embed vignettes, to hide stories within stories, with each story part of a concealed self-sufficiency interlinked and layered into a composite. Through this exercise, I learned how to build novels one narrative at a time.

My writing process presented its own unique challenge. I often struggle with a structured approach; my penchant for rhizomatic thinking and composition takes over. I turn away from graphing, orderliness, drawing boards, mind-mapping, butcher paper, storyboarding, cue cards … Instead, I write like a beacon in the dark, uncertain of where I'm going, but keeping my prose clean and polished as I move forward.

Writing short stories is a journey for me. I usually start with a skeleton, a general idea, and the writing shapes itself. Characters tell their own story and sometimes the story's ending astonishes me. This longer work, however, forced me to be more attentive to structure. Otherwise, I feared, I'd wind up riding a runaway train.

My novel was a thought experiment, but I found myself perfectly at home with made-up characters, places, and even language. For instance:

Myra listens to the fading notes of Amber's song along the boulevard, not understanding a word of it: "*Mah ran en at qu flate vene mondu …*"

"*Pro al fit set Nov,*" joins Tempest in sweet chorus. "*Fo ri zett ob!*"

> The girls have a code between them, a secret language
> that is wonderful and carefree. They call it *pa tabe dome*.
> (187)

Before the novel went public, I longed for my process, my coming to know, to remain raw and unjudged. I called to mind some of my favorite literary novels whose prose lured me like a snake charm.

Vladimir Nabokov's *Lolita* (1955) appealed to me for being as controversial today as it was in 1955. Through half-mad, high-literary ramblings, literature professor Humbert Humbert narrates his obsession and relationship with 12-year-old Dolores Haze—a.k.a. Lolita—or, as Humbert famously alliterates, "my sin, my soul. Lo-lee-ta: the tip of the tongue taking a trip of three steps down the palate to tap, at three, on the teeth. Lo. Lee. Ta" (9). The novel was ahead of its time, breaking ground in unsettling ways to challenge innocence, naturalness, and narrative.

Toni Morrison's *Song of Solomon* (1978) is a work of magic realism enriched by the author's earthy, poetic voice. Fathers fly in ornate clouds and women radiate spells. The protagonist, Macon Milkman, nicknamed for his stretched-out nursing as a child and delayed coming-of-age, is fundamental to the social and racial issues that Morrison unwraps.

Another influential novel was Peter Temple's *Truth* (2009). A review in *The Guardian* refers to it as "tautly constructed and compulsively paced [and] consistently arresting [...] His dialogue is entirely distinctive, full of mangled poetry and beautiful solecisms of ordinary speech. His images can catch in the mind like things glimpsed under lightning" (Gordon). Temple's writing is sharp. Dialogue propels it and, despite much bloodshed, this crime novel is thoroughly literary.

With these authors in mind, I sought out a comparable literary style that rendered my vision, as in this excerpt from Tempest's story in *Claiming T-Mo*:

Now, at six years and a half, Tempest was lofty and shapely enough to pass for twice that age. That day from Nana Salem's, she was inside a yawning field courted on either side by a shadow of trees, halfway toward the community school, when she saw a knot of boys. At first they seemed to be standing, perhaps talking. Then with a shift of moonlight, she realized they were dancing …

Tempest was still meters away when one dancer, the one whose shoulders carried the biggest sway, the one with the richest savage face, disengaged and approached. He was top dog Rock. He took another step toward her and, in a stagger of stilling motion, the rest of them stopped dancing, one by one. They milled beside him.

Tempest stood, a sole girl on a woodlands jaunt, facing hard-core hooligans a dozen strong. Rock parked himself in front of her and whistled.

"Look what we got."

A responding whistle came from the back.

"Oh, my, yes."

"Bit brave, ain't she."

"Bit pretty too."

"Ain't she a scone?"

She picked her way, moved to skirt around them but Rock and the crowd shifted to stand in her path. Her hands balled into fists by her side.

"Feisty!" said Rock. The gang roared, merry.

"She the little freak whose mama's a hybrid," a voice in the back said.

There was a fresh ripple of laughter.

"That true?" Rock eyed her. "You a hybrid?"

"She no hybrid," someone quipped. "She a quarter-brid!"

They roared.

"I never even seen a quarter-brid before. Feel like Columbus!"

They squealed, half-baked sounds like puppy yelps. (171-72)

Later, little Tempest confesses to her parents that she has committed murder. She clutches her father Vida's waist,

her face pressed against his chest, as she trembled and trembled, a six-and-a-half-year-old once more in her daddy's arms.

So they told her stories. Of T-Mo, her grandfather whose night grew silent. Of a girl named Dale Hocking whose pert face and russet tresses wound up in the river bed. Of a man-boy named Al whose body melted to porridge in the water's wash.

Hearing the telling, Myra's voice inside a voice, and seeing Vida's inward drawn eyes, Tempest understood. These were not stories told to reconcile her with what she had done. These were not right or wrong stories. These stories just were. (174)

In my writing, I aspired to channel Morrison's fluidity, her adventurous style and spirit. I pushed boundaries and hoped to immerse readers into the narrative, inviting them to assume the narrator's role and join in the telling.

Influential Critical and Cultural Theories

Postmodernism, gender theory, narratology, and psycho-analytic thinking informed my project. In particular, I borrowed from Simone de Beauvoir's concepts of ambiguity, embodiment, the self, and otherness, and I foregrounded the challenges and possibilities of being different, of being in/between worlds.

Towards a feminist critique. *Claiming T-Mo* features strong female characters (namely Silhouette, Myra, and Tempest) who counter the marginalization of women against dominant ideologies of male supremacy. Feminist theory critically reassesses the patriarchal social order, addressing themes of disempowerment (e.g., Salem, betrothed as a child bride) and empowerment (e.g., Tempest, a storm in her fist). I wanted my females to challenge the gendered status quo.

The postmodern impetus. Broadly speaking, a literary, speculative, Russian-doll-style novel like *Claiming T-Mo* can be understood as a work of postmodernist fiction insofar as it is playful, fragmented, intertextual, and metareferential, breaking "boundaries between different discourses, between fiction and nonfiction, history and autobiography" (Carter 119).

Postmodernism may be an exhausted late twentieth-century phenomenon; it's difficult to say where the cultural landscape currently stands. Only in retrospect do these formations take shape. Whatever the case, I like the freedom of postmodern thinking. Specifically, I'm attracted to the way it encourages hybridization and inclusiveness—a marriage of writings, Barthes would say. Hence my embedded (i.e., married) stories form a new, dynamic whole. But Barthes is referring to more than this general association; he means the non-originality of the text, its interdependence on other literary texts, whereby a text is a multidimensional space assembled by writers who pre-mix, borrow from, and draw upon what has already been written. According to Barthes: "The Text is not a co-existence of meanings but a passage, an overcrossing; thus it answers not to an interpretation, even a liberal one, but to an explosion, a dissemination" (158). Barthes emphasizes the role of readers in this equation. Whereas the writer brings the text to life by composing it, readers co-author the text by bringing their own ideas and perceptions to the experience.

Barthes' idealized postmodern reader, then, does not approach the text as a passive bystander but as an active participant shaped by subjectivity, personal experience, and cultural inscription. Like the author, this reader recognizes that "our realities are infused with fictions, and that stories are not lies but monuments to the search for a specifically human truth" (Ommundsen 106). In the realm of postmodernism, "truth" is an illusion, of course, and it should always be enclosed in quotes. The journey is the thing. What matters is the search for newness—for original, innovative modes of thought, style, and meaning that convey more nuanced expressions of the "true" human condition. *Claiming T-Mo* operates within this sphere of influence.

Perception and difference. Simone de Beauvoir was a woman before her time. In books like *The Ethics of Ambiguity* (1945) and *The Second Sex* (1949), she addresses themes of otherness, alterity, embodiment, disclosure, temporality, and place. Her ideas about perception and difference in particular were instrumental to the development of my characters.

Claiming T-Mo suggests that alterity arises from a relational means of identification. When one parent is "non-human" and the other is human, the offspring (e.g., Myra or Tempest) find themselves in a position of being inside and outside simultaneously. They inhabit both worlds but are predominantly outside. This being-outside is not confined to "human" DNA; it includes perception. Even the fully human Vida finds himself ostracized from his peers. During childhood, he is perceived as "different" because of his frail physical stature and poor health. When young Vida laughs with the children who shun him, he is trying to find agency, to elevate his marginalized status as an insider/outsider. It doesn't work. Time and experience give him wisdom of perspective. The older Vida teaches his child Tempest that "difference" has no organic connection to identity or being. Rather, like truth and reality, it is a matter of perception.

On narratology. As I explain in *Writing Speculative Fiction* (2019), "narratology is both a method of inquiry and a modern literary theory. It relates to a school of thought, a humanistic discipline generally associated with the term. It also refers to the study of narrative structure, closely linked to the study of rhetoric, structuralism and semiotics" (149).

Werner Wolf refers to narratology as a literary discipline applicable in verbal and other remote media, such as graphics, photography, film, music, radio, and drama (146). In literary theory, narratology relates to the study of narrative structure and is closely linked to structuralism and semiotics. Tzvetan Todorov calls it the "science of narrative," an instrument for codifying texts (10). It has been variously referred to as a school of thought, but for me, "narratology" is more of a mode of representation.

In *Writing Fiction* (2007), Amanda Boulter discusses how readers identify a distinct voice in an author's phrases, repetitions, pauses, and other intricacies. Especially distinctive is the dialogue between characters: their different languages, values, differences, and points of view. Readers' inner ears bring to life an author's imagined voice. Without the work of readers, argues Boulter, there is no fiction; readers are "ventriloquists" through which authors speaks (69).

Boulter references Seymour Chatman's diagram of narrative text. "Chatman charts several stages between the actual writer (in this book, me) and the actual reader (you)" (71). His diagram begins with the real author, then moves through a number of other filters, including the implied author, narrator, narratee, and implied reader. The diagram culminates in the real reader. "The 'implied reader' was a term first coined by Wayne Booth in the early 1960s as a way of describing (or imagining) the kind of reader the author had in mind when they were writing" (72). This reader "is, in other words, the writer's voice. And the writer's voice, like everything else in fiction, can only be 'heard' and brought to life by the reader. But just as the reader is inventing the author, so the author is inventing the reader" (73).

In *Claiming T-Mo*, my implied reader is a version of my implied author (i.e., "me"), who understands and enjoys fiction that breaks rules and aspires for genuine innovation. By extension, the real author is a version of this implied author, but she doesn't matter: she's just a medium through which the "people" that matter fabricate my narrative artifact.

Psychoanalysis and Characterization. Psychoanalytic principles undergird the characters in *Claiming T-Mo*, who embody dominant archetypes (i.e., hero, shadow, shapeshifter, etc.). I mainly took cues from Freud and Jung. Freudian concepts like the dynamic unconscious and the Oedipus complex allowed me to show how repressed memories and desires can well up and (re)determine our perceptions and behavior. With respect to archetypes, Jung's conception of the collective unconscious provided additional guidance.

I tried to illustrate what Jung calls "individuation," "a process by which the individual is helped to harmonize his/her 'persona' (the self as presented to the world) and 'the shadow' (the darker potentially dangerous side of the personality that exists in the personal unconscious" (Carter 80). To varying degrees, all of the characters in the novel give off light and shade. As such, the novel engages with difference and, I hope, prompts readers to think more deeply about difference.

What the Examiners Saw

After my Ph.D. supervisor, Dr. Dominique Hecq, endorsed my creative dissertation, I had to wait to receive feedback from additional examiners. Here are some of their comments:

Examiner 1

Summary: The portfolio is a praiseworthy and intellectually valuable submission, and is certainly of Ph.D. standard […] There are some slight emendations suggested in my report that would help the portfolio. I would not wish to insist on any of them, only that they be considered […] This is a reflection only of the complexity and interest of the project, which sparked a lot of ideas in me as a reader […] more that I wanted to unpack it further. This is an admirable piece of work. The novel is, I believe, publishable, and the exegesis ranges widely and fruitfully. Both were a pleasure to read.

Assessment: The portfolio includes a novel [...] and an accompanying exegesis. It is a wide-ranging, provocative, and intellectually satisfying project that contains a novel of publishable quality and accompanying essay that usefully and articulately interrogates the process of writing, both generally and personally. The novel is, in general terms, an interlinked series of short stories. However, the intention of the work is to take the strengths of the short story—impact, succinctness, emphasis—and marry that to the wider and more discursive arc of a novel. This it achieves handsomely.

Examiner 2

Summary: The changes I am recommending are restricted to the exegesis [...] The novel is an exemplary manuscript. Though not yet (I suspect) ready for publication, it is ambitious and energetic; written with passion and vibrancy, the novel is notable for its engaging voice and robust female characters, as well as its nuanced and sensual engagement with mothering and caring. I recommend that the novel remain untouched.

Assessment: The novel is, I think, a beautiful, if wobbly, masterpiece. It is full of energy, ambition, wit, and heart. The characters, imagery, and themes are robust and lively. Many of the scenes are evoked with a poeticism that enlivens character, opens the heart, offers strangeness in a way that is both alluring and engaging. The exegesis is, I think, rich in terms of the broad scope of theoretical ideas with which it engages. It is enthusiastic and generous in the way it engages with ideas and practices. There is clear evidence here of a wide reading, of a dedication to the challenge of learning how to read and write academically. The exegesis has a confident, sometimes even arrogant, swagger to it.

What the Reader Saw

How does a reader decipher a text? In *Metafictions? Reflexivity in Contemporary Texts* (1993), Wenche Ommundsen discusses refiguring the narrative act:

Unlike "normal" face-to-face conversation, literature does not involve the simultaneous presence of both sender and addressee; and the context, so important to the meaning of most verbal acts, is unstable. The reader is absent from the scene of writing, thus unable to provide feedback, and at the time of reading, the author is not there to ensure that we get the "correct" message. The author cannot truly legislate for the reception of her/ his text: we can only guess at how Shakespeare intended us to understand his work but must assume that the passing of time and the multiplication of readers have affected its intelligibility in important ways. (57)

I heeded Ommundsen's point that the reader was absent from the writing and did not have the privilege of the author's presence at the time of the reading. This meant that the reader did not come to the text with an explicit knowledge of my intentions, capabilities, psyche, historical realities, world views, or moral concepts. The reader did not arrive with access to my notes, drafts, and proof corrections to accurately interpret my authorial intent. Even if readers did arrive with some insight, they tugged along their own psyche, historical realities, world views, and moral concepts that influenced the act of reading.

Of course, it was pointless to fret about whether my readers were getting the "correct" message. My archetypal characters were flexible, complex, and unpredictable—they would always-already inhabit a chronic state of evolution, changing in tandem with the various subjectivities and perceptions that gazed at them. "The literary act is a collective effort," Ommundsen writes.

> Like most human relationships, literary communication mediates a precarious balance of power: power to narrate, power to interpret, power, finally, to accept or decline the roles offered by one's partners in the literary act" (68). Writing is a form of funambulism. As an author, I walk across a tightrope between multiple conditioning factors in the author/reader relationship that hinge on how the reader interacts with the text.
>
> I remained wary of this dynamic, as "authors can never allow themselves to forget that readers possess the supreme power, which is that of abandoning the text. The author must exercise textual authority in such a way as to ensure that this will not happen. Not surprisingly, then, textual communication is frequently represented as an act of love: the text must offer itself as an object of desire, seduce the reader, play and be played upon like the body of a lover" (71).

Reviews of *Claiming T-Mo*

The publisher loved the style of the book. Later, critics and reviewers had their say. Below are a few excerpts:

"Much of the story is these interwoven threads, all related to one another but telling the story from a variety of perspectives. In this way, they pull together a richly woven tapestry of the story, supplemented by the gorgeous and lush language. The voices of each of the multitude of characters are distinct and evocative, painting an entire picture of each character within a few brief pages of their introduction. And while many of the events of the book are clearly from the realm of speculative fiction, the story is told in such a way that it all seems real." —*Mad Scientist Journal*

"Bacon employs elegant and poetic language that pulls readers into each different world and experience as felt by the three leading women. Recommended reading for those with an interest in sf, expressive language, and stories that focus on women's relationships and perspectives." —*Library Journal*

"*Claiming T-Mo* takes readers on a breathless journey through kaleidoscopic worlds that resemble the mythic veins and sinews of our own, pulsing with unalloyed vitality. Within this visceral, shimmering universe, beautifully drawn characters spin their intersecting tales in language that bristles with visionary exuberance. And throughout looms the presence—and absence—of the mercurial and mysterious T-Mo, who alone holds the answers to questions that lie too deep to be asked. As playful as it is thought-provoking, this is a work of dizzying originality and profound humanity." —Oz Hardwick, award-winning poet and academic

"*Claiming T-Mo* is a story of generations of women striving for fulfillment, but caught in webs of passion, magic and stardust. Eugen Bacon embraces the strange and estranged in this unanticipated contemporary trickster myth." —Emmet O'Cuana, author of *Faraway*

"Although there are elements of fantasy, science fiction, magic, hybrid characters, interplanetary travel and shape-shifting characters in this enthralling story, it is its thought-provoking complexity and its essential humanity which make it so much more than the sum of these labels. [Bacon's] explorations of how people discover who they are, how they manage to cope with difference, to discover their inner strengths and how they learn to understand and to relate to others, are central to the development of the story. Through her characters she highlights that, whoever you are, and wherever you come from, the need to find your place in your world, and to find loving relationships, is a universal quest." —*NB Magazine*

"Bacon's whole book feels itself like a fairytale, albeit one where mystical planets and traveling between stars take the place of castles and sorcery. That said, there is a peculiar witchcraft at work in *Claiming T-Mo*. It resembles the writing of NK Jemisin, particularly in the way it nests the human in the fantastic, and it incorporates the kind of galaxy-spanning scope of generations once used by Octavia E. Butler. Simultaneously lean and lush, it's a book that's more inquisitive about the limitless thematic and tonal possibilities of science fiction than the genre of science fiction as such." —*NPR*

Coda

The production of *Claiming T-Mo* entailed writing/being different and adopting the short-story and speculative forms as I explored themes of in/betweenness. I experienced a wealth of emotions during the process, ranging from high anxiety to deep-seated fulfillment, and I found that I adopted certain aspects of my characters; the more I immersed myself in their worlds, the more I constructed their realities, perceptions, and desires—the more I inhabited *a state of becoming myself.* I came to love my characters, who talked to me, whose stories began to tell themselves, and who ultimately provided me with a safe space to better define the contours of my own identity.

But knowledge is always retrospective. I still want answers, especially to those questions I have yet to ask …

References

Bacon, Eugen. *Claiming T-Mo*. Meerkat Press, 2019.

———. *Writing Speculative Fiction*. Red Globe Press, 2019.

Barthes, Roland. "From Work to Text." 1971. *Image, Music, Text*. Fontana Press, 1977.

———. *The Grain of the Voice: Interviews (1962-1980)*. Hill & Wang, 1985.

Boulter, Amanda. *Writing Fiction: Creative and Critical Approaches*. Palgrave Macmillan, 2007.

Carter, David. *Literary Theory*. Oldcastle Books, 2006.

Deleuze, Gilles and Fèlix Guattari. *A Thousand Plateaus.* 1980. Trans. Brian Massumi. University of Minnesota Press, 1987.

Gordon, Edmund. "*Truth* by Peter Temple." *The Guardian*. January 9, 2010. Online. Accessed November 19, 2021.

Lovell, Bronwyn, 2020. "Men Claiming Women and Women Claiming Their Strength." *TEXT: Journal of Writing and*

Writing Courses 24.1 (April): 1-19.

Montiglio, Silvia. *From Villain to Hero: Odysseus in Ancient Thought.* University of Michigan Press, 2011.

Nabokov, Vladimir. *Lolita.* 1995. Vintage, 1997.

Ommundsen, Wenche. *Metafictions? Reflexivity in Contemporary Texts.* Melbourne University Press, 1993.

Todorov, Tzvetan. *Grammaire du Décaméron.* Mouton, 1969.

Vogler, Christopher. *The Writer's Journey.* Michael Wiese, 1998.

Wolf, Werner. "Narratology and Media(lity): The Transmedial Expansion of a Literary Discipline and Possible Consequences." *Current Trends in Narratology.* De Gruyter, 2011.

EUGEN BACON is an African Australian author of several novels and fiction collections as well as *Writing Speculative Fiction*. In 2023, *An Earnest Blackness* received the British Fantasy Award for Best Nonfiction, and the book was a finalist for the Locus and Ditmar Awards. Bacon's books have also been nominated for or won the British Science Fiction Association Award, Foreword Indies Award, Bridport Prize, Copyright Agency Prize, Horror Writers Association Diversity Grant, Otherwise Fellowship, Nommo Award, and others. Her creative work has appeared in *Award Winning Australian Writing, Fantasy Magazine, Year's Best African Speculative Fiction*, and *Fantasy & Science Fiction*. Visit Bacon's website at **eugenbacon.com**.

Milton Keynes UK
Ingram Content Group UK Ltd.
UKHW011440031123
431729UK00004B/138

9 798986 547954